THIS IS A CARLTON BOOK

Published in 2019 by Carlton Books Limited
20 Mortimer Street, London W1T 3JW

© & ™ 2019 Lucasfilm Ltd

A catalogue record for this book is available
from the British Library.

ISBN: 978 1 84796 102 0

Editorial Director: Roland Hall
Design: Russell Knowles
Production: Rachel Burgess
Book and app concept created by Japhet Asher

CONTENTS

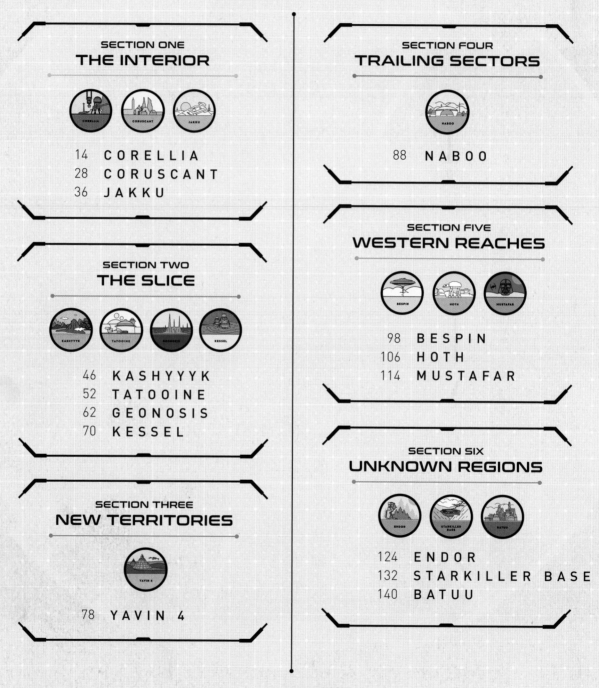

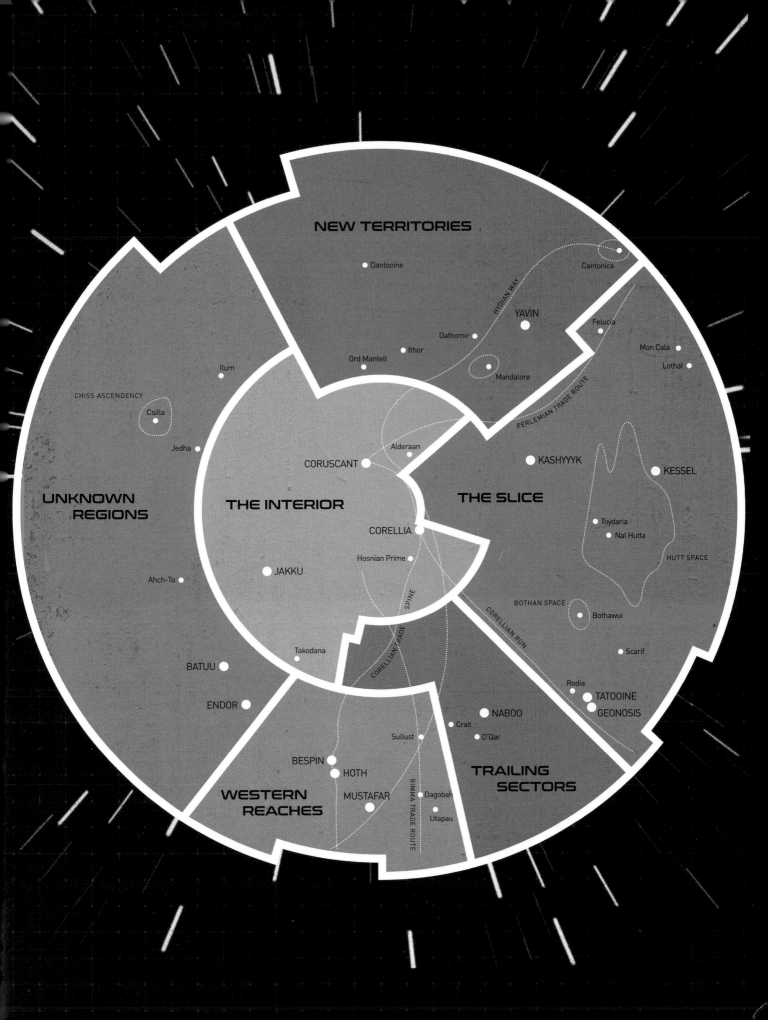

HOW TO USE

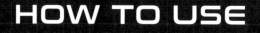

THE GALATIC EXPLORER'S GUIDE

DOWNLOAD THE

STAR WARS AR BOOK HOLOSCANNER APP

FROM YOUR LOCAL
APPLE, GOOGLE OR ANDROID
APP STORE
AND OPEN IT ON YOUR
SMART DEVICE.

Download on the App Store

GET IT ON Google Play

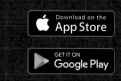

FOLLOW ON-SCREEN INSTRUCTIONS TO SET UP YOUR *STAR WARS* HOLOSCANNER AND UNLOCK AMAZING INTERACTIVE SIMULATIONS OF WEAPONS, VEHICLES, CREATURES AND INFORMATION FROM ACROSS THE GALAXY.

LOOK FOR THE HOLOSCANNER SYMBOL ON SPECIAL TRIGGER PAGES IN THE GUIDE.

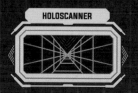

HOLOSCANNER

SCAN PAGES WITH THE HOLOSCANNER SYMBOL BY POINTING YOUR DEVICE AT THE WHOLE PAGE. THIS WILL REVEAL AN AUGMENTED REALITY LAYER IN FULL 3D.

GREETINGS, GALACTIC EXPLORE

YOU HAVE MADE A WISE CHOICE IN SELECTING THIS GUIDE FC
JOURNEY. BOOKS ARE RARE ACROSS THE GALAXY, AND THIS ONE I
STILL. IT COMBINES THE WISDOM AND EXPERIENCE OF PIRATE AND PF
MERCHANT AND MERCENARY, DARTH AND DROID IN ONE EXTRAO
VOLUME OF PLANETARY LORE. AS MY SWEET MOTHER USED TO SAY, I
TO KNOW WHAT YOU DON'T KNOW.

Each planet's most significant locations are highlighted, alongside
momentous events that have taken place there. This includes
battle sites, birthplaces, secret base locations and other, more
mysterious, knowledge on local customs, wildlife and long forgotter
lore. A galactic explorer who wished to visit a planet would finc
this information more than useful; an armchair explorer will finc
it essential. As a pirate, I am quite happy to accept your paymen
either way.

More than this, the *Galactic Explorer's Guide* combines the seen anc
the unseen, the known and the unknown. The book contains hidder
hololayers of knowledge and experience for you to discover. Use the
holoscanner we have provided to summon BB-8 to you to join you
journey. And that's just the beginning.

With your holoscanner, you can examine details of famous craft like
the X-wing and the *Millennium Falcon* as they float above the page
Learn to fire blasters and bowcasters. Fight a wave of battle droids
Project a map of the galaxy's planets in the space around you anc
explore. You may find hidden surprises and secrets out there. You
may even find me.

If you do, I'll share more about myself and my plans. There may ever
be a way we can help a common cause...

For now, though, let me introduce a droid I've obtained and specially
programmed to provide suitable commentary on your destinations
He's called DK-RA-43 and is a former protocol droid, who I hope wil
therefore remember his manners. He certainly will, if he remember

"I have been ordered to assist presumably because my databanks contain more information about the galaxy than any organic being's brain could possibly hold. Since you're wondering, I began my existence as an RA-7 protocol droid, built for the Empire in the great droid factories of Affa. Or maybe you weren't wondering – I find organics tend to be curious only about subjects that are unimportant, distasteful or both.

My current master tells me he acquired me in a sabacc game, though sometimes he says it was in exchange for a purebred Loth-cat and a barrel of Savareen brandy. To be honest, my master says a lot of things, particularly if he's been at Oga's Cantina for too long. After my last memory wipe, he outfitted me with databases he acquired from several top-of-the-line tourism droids.

To aid you as you explore the galaxy, I have been ordered to prepare dossiers about a number of planets he says we may visit, as well as a few he says we won't actually go to. I found that confusing. Some of these worlds, quite frankly, are unsuitable for a visit by civilized people because they are extremely dangerous. Others would only be visited by someone with a keen interest in wreckage or ruins. When I pointed this out, my master threatened me with another memory wipe. But between us, my databases have information about hundreds of worlds that would be far more enjoyable as vacation spots than the ones my master has chosen. Let me know and we will soon be on our way to somewhere far more interesting and relaxing. My master also directed me to include information in these dossiers that I don't see why any normal explorer or tourist would want to know. Hence the descriptions of ancient battles, local transport, and unpleasant resident fauna that I highly advise not to encounter in person.

My master may not have briefed either of us fully. He tends to be short on details, probably because there are Ikadrian flitter-whipits with longer attention spans than his. It's also possible that he will involve us in one of his schemes, one he thinks will allow him to be even richer and lazier than he already is. If that's the case, I sincerely hope it does not go wrong – as tends to happen with my master's plans. I wouldn't like to find us locked in a detention cell, clapped into shackles by Zygerrians, or sentenced to hard labor in the spice mines of Kessel.

Though if we do wind up in the spice mines of Kessel, when we're not breaking rocks I'll be able to recite facts from the dossier I prepared about

THE GALAXY

TECHNOLOGY IS A WONDERFUL THING: IT UNITES THE SCATTERED PLANETS ACROSS THE GALAXY AND THE DIVERSE SPECIES OF SENTIENT LIFE FROM HUMANS TO JAWAS, WOOKIEES TO EWOKS AND HUTTS. WITHOUT THE HYPERDRIVE, THERE WOULD BE NO GALACTIC EMPIRE, REBEL ALLIANCE, OUTER RIM OR FIRST ORDER. THERE WOULD SIMPLY BE THE VAST STARFIELD OF SPACE.

The galaxy today is an enormous, dangerous place. The histories can make each region sound like little more than a battlefield, littered with carcasses of burned out battle cruisers and defeated armies. But life goes on in even the most remote and desolate places, even those that now only live in memory. The real galaxy is hidden from easy view, behind masks, in memories, rumors and shadows. A true galactic explorer will seek out what is hidden, whatever the challenge. Nothing is impossible to find. There are established trade routes, secure spaceports and reliable transport if you know where to look and who to ask...

The stories of the Empire and the Rebel Alliance, the First Order and the Resistance are legend. But the lifeblood of planets across the galaxy is in the hands of those who may not be what they seem. A trader can moonlight as a bounty hunter. A smuggler might also be a rebel operative. Even a droid may have been sliced and reprogrammed to hide its real mission.

So keep your eyes and ears open, use your holoscanner and follow instructions carefully – you may find the forces that shape the galaxy are already closer than you think...

HOLOSCANNER

CORELLIA

CORUSCANT

JAKKU

KASHYYYK

TATOOINE

GEONOSIS

KESSEL

YAVIN 4

NABOO

BESPIN

HOTH

MUSTAFAR

ENDOR

STARKILLER BASE

BATUU

THE INTERIOR

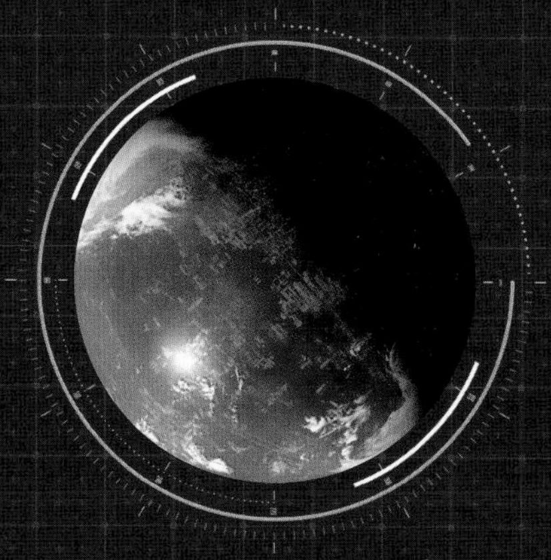

CORELLIA

Early Corellians were among the galaxy's most daring explorers, and their homeworld was a power in the ancient Republic. But its importance has diminished and the planet is now mired in pollution and poverty, with only its massive shipyards recalling its past glories.

CORUSCANT

Believed to be the birthplace of humanity, Coruscant was the pinnacle of galactic power and culture for millennia. After the fall of the Empire, criminal syndicates rose to power, leaving Coruscant a tarnished world where only the rich can afford security.

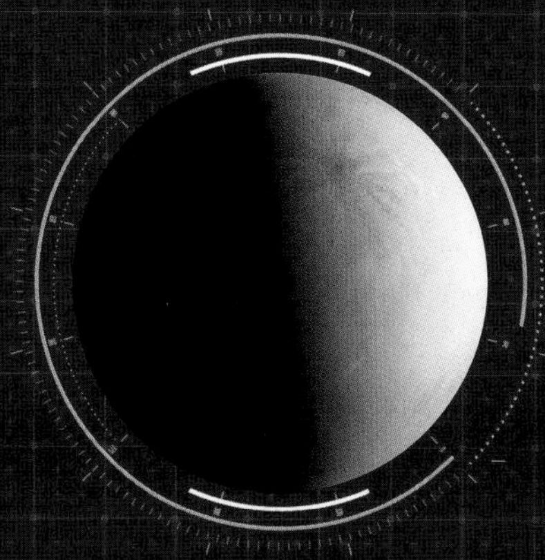

JAKKU

A bleak desert world on the frontier, Jakku was the site of a climactic battle between the New Republic and the Empire's remnants, a ferocious confrontation that left the planet's sands littered with the wreckage of downed capital ships, fighters and ground vehicles.

NEW TERRITORIES

THE INTERIOR

THE SLICE

UNKNOWN REGIONS

WESTERN REACHES

TRAILING SECTORS

CHISS ASCENDENCY

HUTT SPACE

BOTHAN SPACE

Dantooine

Cantonica

HYDIAN WAY

Yavin

Dathomir

Felucia

Mon Cala

Lothal

Ithor

Ord Mantell

Mandalore

PERLEMIAN TRADE ROUTE

Ilum

Csilla

Alderaan

Kashyyyk

Kessel

CORUSCANT

Jedha

Toydaria

Nal Hutta

CORELLIA

Hosnian Prime

Ahch-To

JAKKU

CORELLIAN RUN

Bothawui

Scarif

SPINE

Batuu

Takodana

Rodia

Tatooine

Geonosis

CORELLIAN TRADE

Endor

Naboo

Crait

D'Qar

Sullust

Bespin

Hoth

RIMMA TRADE ROUTE

Dagobah

Mustafar

Utapau

HOLOSCANNER

REVEAL THE
3D GALAXY MAP

CORELLIA

PLANETARY DATA

SECTOR: Corellian

TYPE: Terrestrial

CLIMATE: Temperate

DIAMETER: 11,000 km

TERRAIN: Hills, forests, plains

ROTATION PERIOD: 25 standard hours

ORBITAL PERIOD: 329 local rotations

SENTIENT SPECIES: Humans

POPULATION: 3 billion

SECTION ONE

CORELLIA

THOUSANDS OF YEARS AGO CORELLIANS BLAZED MANY OF THE GALAXY'S MOST CRITICAL HYPERSPACE ROUTES, AND THE WORLD'S COLONISTS SETTLED THOUSANDS OF PLANETS, MAKING CORELLIA A KEY WORLD IN THE REPUBLIC. BUT THAT WAS MILLENNIA AGO, BEFORE GALACTIC POWER SHIFTED TO YOUNGER, MORE VIBRANT WORLDS, LEAVING CORELLIA A POLLUTED PLANET WITH A REPUTATION FOR POVERTY AND CRIME. CORELLIA HAS REMAINED A SHIPBUILDING POWER, HOWEVER, WITH THE EMPIRE NATIONALIZING ITS INDUSTRIES TO SERVE ITS WAR MACHINE. CORELLIAN SHIPYARDS BUILT SOME OF THE FASTEST WARSHIPS IN THE IMPERIAL NAVY. THIS MARK OF DISTINCTION BECAME A SOURCE OF PRIDE FOR ITS DOWNTRODDEN PEOPLE, DESPITE THEIR RESENTMENT OF THE EMPIRE.

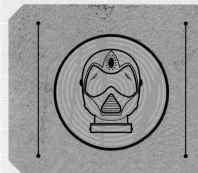

DK-RA-43'S COMMENT

There's so much history on Corellia! Too bad it's such an awful place, filled with thieving urchins, ruthless gangs and murderous slavers. And even honest Corellians – if you can find them – drive hard bargains and are always looking for an angle. If Corellian culture is what we're after, I can prepare dossiers on 611 colony worlds that offer authentic cultural experiences but substantially less chance of being assaulted, robbed, or killed.

OVERVIEW

CORONET CITY • CORONA HOUSE • TREASURE SHIP ROW • DORISMUS ATHENAEUM • TYRENA • DOABA GUERFEL • GOLD BEACHES • ORIK'S SPINE • KEEN'S GROTTO

HISTORY

Wanderlust has always been a Corellian trait. Ancient Corellians sailed the planet's storm-tossed oceans and colonized worlds beyond the galactic frontier, and the planet remains known for its hyperspace scouts.

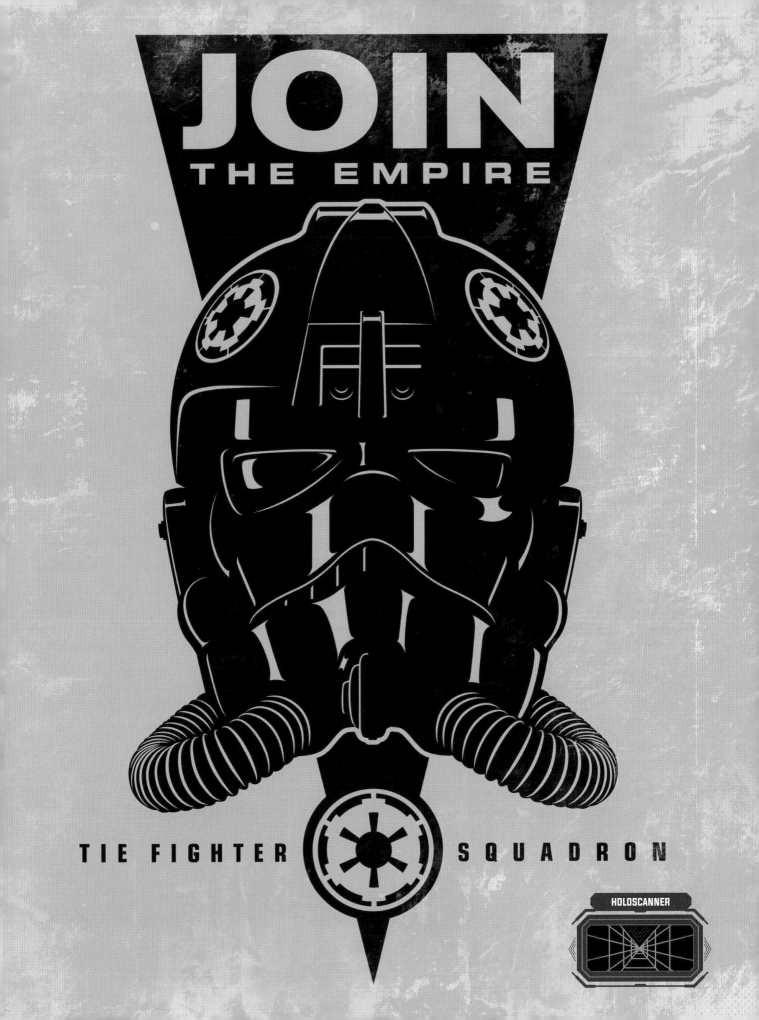

VEHICLES

M-68 LANDSPEEDER

Constructed as both a hardtop and an open-air model, Mobquet's M-68 is hailed as a classic by street racers and speeder aficionados alike. From the 289-hirep repulsorlift generator (which any astromech can overcharge) to the powerful injectrine engines and their variable exhaust thruster nozzles, the M-68 is one mean machine.

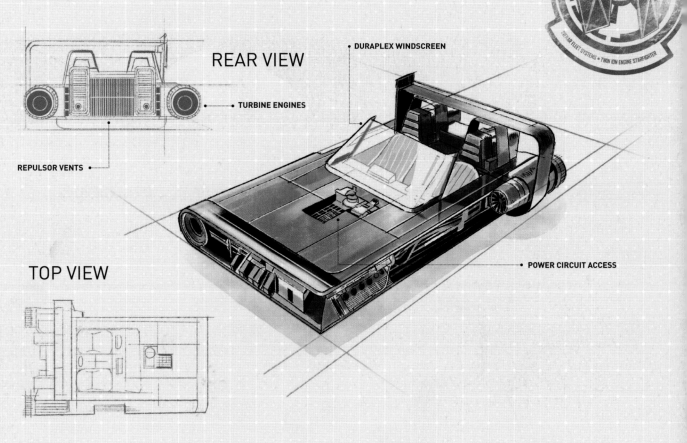

REAR VIEW

DURAPLEX WINDSCREEN

TURBINE ENGINES

REPULSOR VENTS

TOP VIEW

POWER CIRCUIT ACCESS

LIVE FAST, DIE YOUNG

If it has an engine or motor, expect a Corellian to see how fast it can go – and another Corellian to try and make it go faster. Corellians have always been avid racers, breeding animals, tinkering with machines and betting on races. Illegal swoop races are a nightly menace on Coronet City's streets, and even legal events are viciously no-holds-barred affairs. One of the most famous races (with a body count to match) is the annual Orik's Spine Challenge.

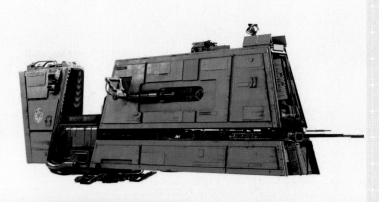

SPECIES

GRINDALIDS

Grindalids hail from Persis IX, a gloomy, cloud-covered world in the Expansion Region, but have become mainstays of Coronet City's underworld, with gangs such as the infamous White Worms controlling large chunks of the black market. Grindalid skin burns in sunlight, so these wormlike beings are rarely seen above ground without protective gear. They prefer to conduct business in dank lairs beneath the streets of their adopted city.

CREATURES

SIBIAN HOUNDS

These hairless quadrupeds come in a variety of breeds, none of which is known for its beauty. Sibian hounds are ideal hunters and watchbeasts, combining a keen sense of smell with speed and agility. They are often thought of as vicious, but this reputation is unfair: Sibians are gentle and loyal if trained by a kind master.

HOLOSCANNER

CORELLIAN UNDERWORLD

Coronet City's gaudy Treasure Ship Row is an open-air bazaar that's operated since the time when Corellian sea captains settled disputes with swords and whips, and is one of many neighborhoods rich in history. But beneath such wealthy districts lie labyrinths of sewers and tunnels. This subterranean realm is the territory of criminal gangs such as the White Worms, the SuperNovas and the Black Fleeks.

INTRODUCING
The Millennium
FALCON

EPIC STARSHIP

THE *MILLENNIUM FALCON*

She may look dilapidated, but the *Millennium Falcon* has it where it counts, thanks to Han Solo's modifications. Han flew the *Falcon* from Kessel to Savareen, making the Kessel Run in less than 12 parsecs, then won the freighter from Lando Calrissian in a sabacc game. Since then, the *Falcon* has seen action at Yavin, Endor, Starkiller Base, and Crait.

CONCUSION MISSILE TUBES

QUAD LASER CANNON

FORWARD MANDIBLES

EQUIPMENT ACCESS BAY

DEFLECTOR SHIELD PROJECTOR

SENSOR DISH

FORWARD FLOODLIGHT

QUAD LASER CANNON

COCKPIT

ARMOR PLATING

DRIVE UNITS

TOP VIEW

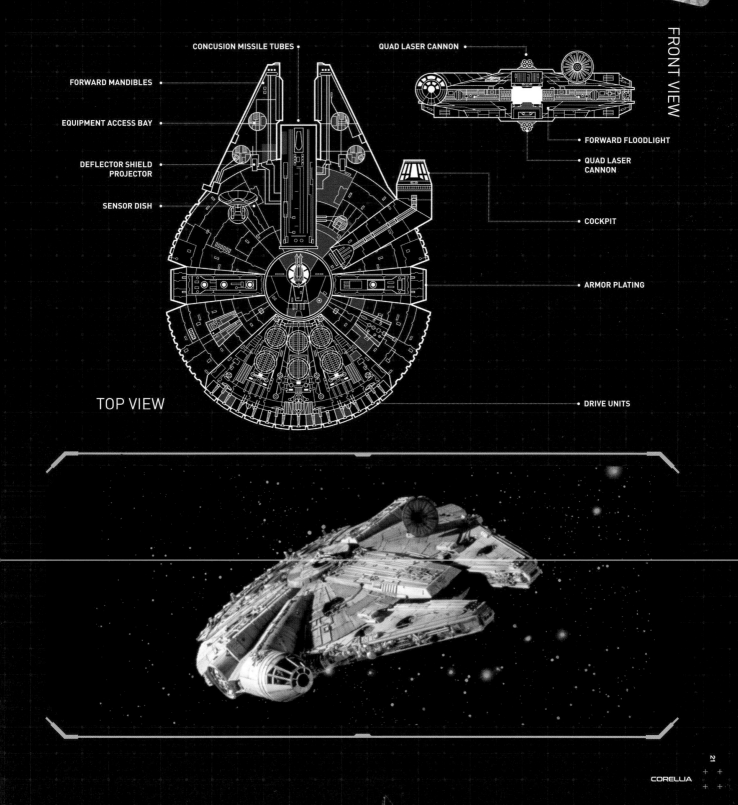

HOLOSCANNER

FLY THE
MILLENNIUM FALCON

YT-1300 LIGHT FREIGHTER
1,050 KM/H
ISU-SIM SSP05 HYPERDRIVE
QUADEX POWER CORE
34.75M LONG

MILLENNIUM FALCON
YT-1300f LIGHT FREIGHTER

VEHICLE PRODUCTION

TIE STRIKER

A design that emerged from the Empire's Scarif think tank, the TIE striker was built for atmospheric patrols over ground-based installations. While never a favorite of the Admiralty, forward-thinking commanders came to appreciate the TIE striker's combination of speed and armament, leading to a steady stream of orders from shipyards such as Corellia's.

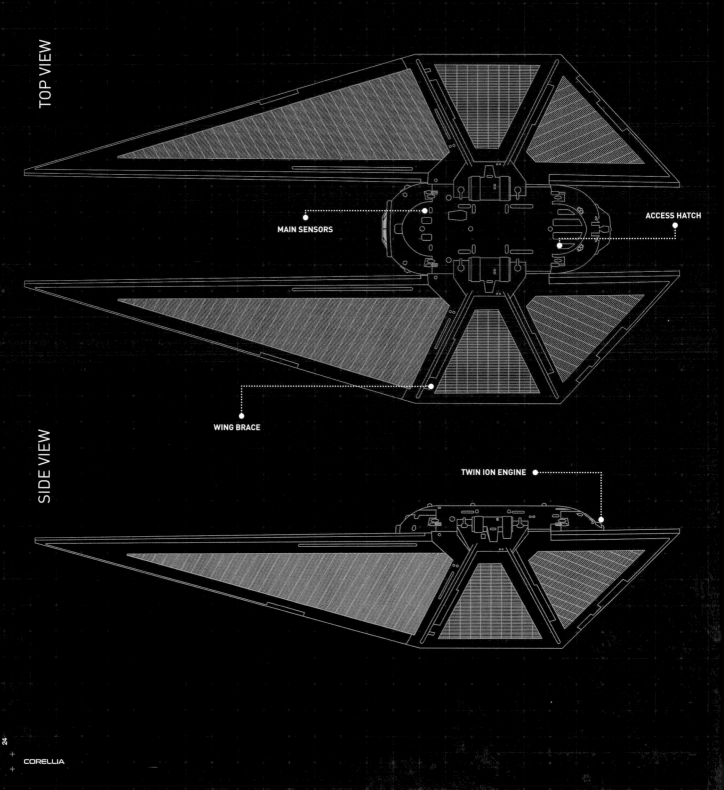

TOP VIEW

MAIN SENSORS

ACCESS HATCH

WING BRACE

SIDE VIEW

TWIN ION ENGINE

IMPERIAL CARGO SHUTTLE

The Empire nationalized many of Corellia's shipyards to produce everything from capital ships and starfighters to the utilitarian vehicles that keep its supply lines running. The *Zeta*-class shuttle is a versatile cargo hauler that transports modular cargo pods beneath its belly. These cargo shuttles are flown by Imperial pilots as well as civilian contractors.

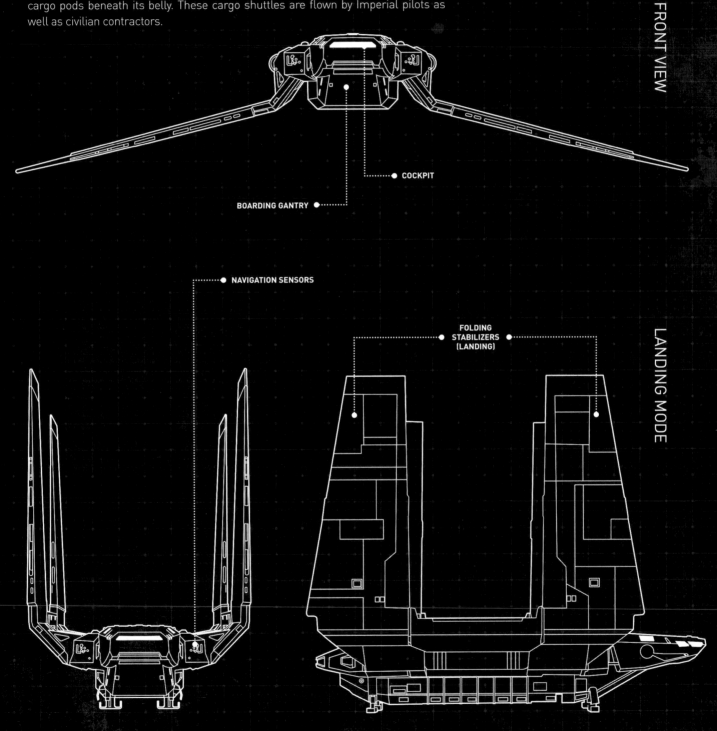

COCKPIT

BOARDING GANTRY

NAVIGATION SENSORS

FOLDING STABILIZERS (LANDING)

HAN SOLO

Equally famous as a rebel hero and a cocky smuggler, Han Solo escaped his dismal youth as a Coronet City scrumrat by enlisting in the Imperial Navy. Han's Imperial career was brief: he washed out as a cadet and deserted the infantry, but earned a dishonest living alongside Chewbacca aboard the *Millennium Falcon*.

QI'RA

Above all else a survivor, Qi'ra survived growing up in the Silo, one of Corellia's grimmest neighborhoods, to become a scrumrat with the White Worms and then a rising star in Crimson Dawn, which rewarded her organizational skills, combat prowess and ruthlessness when tested.

WEDGE ANTILLES

Han Solo wasn't the only Corellian to become a rebel hero. Wedge Antilles deserted the Empire to take up with the Alliance, surviving the battles of Yavin and Hoth to lead a squadron at Endor, where he helped take down the second Death Star. He then flew with the New Republic, training a new generation of pilots on Hosnian Prime.

LADY PROXIMA

The Grindalid matriarch of the White Worms, Lady Proxima oversaw a web of criminal operations from her lair in the lightless sewers of Corellia's Coronet City. Proxima hated Han Solo, who had betrayed her and injured her by exposing her to sunlight. She spent many years seeking revenge on the former scrumrat turned smuggler and rebel hero.

LEGENDARY SHIPYARDS

Corellians have been shipbuilders and pilots for millennia, and Coronet City's vast shipyards occupy the same sites where ocean-going vessels were once built. Companies such as the legendary Corellian Engineering Corporation are famous across the galaxy for creating everything from freighters to warships. The Empire nationalized Corellia's shipyards to produce TIE fighters and Star Destroyers, with Corellian-made Star Destroyers winning a reputation as the fastest in their class.

DROIDS

L-1G WORKER DROIDS

Corellia's shipyards and factories employ thousands of organics, but they must compete for work with worker droids that perform dangerous and tedious jobs without complaint. Models such as the L-1g are resented by humans and others looking for a way out of poverty.

WEAPON

SCRUMRAT STAFF

Violence in Corellia's underworld is fueled by a brisk trade in stolen blasters and vibroblades, but Corellian criminals also carry improvised weapons which are easier to slip past security scanners. The scrumrat Rebolt carried a staff made from a snapped transmission mast, and connected it to a power cell that gave an extra jolt to anyone unlucky enough to be on the receiving end.

365

CORUSCANT

PLANETARY DATA

SECTOR: Corusca

TYPE: Terrestrial

CLIMATE: Temperate

DIAMETER: 12,240 km

TERRAIN: Urban cityscape

ROTATION PERIOD: 24 standard hours

ORBITAL PERIOD: 365 local rotations

SENTIENT SPECIES: Humans

POPULATION: 1 trillion

CORUSCANT

THE HEART OF GALACTIC CIVILIZATION, CORUSCANT IS A CITY THAT COVERS AN ENTIRE PLANET, WITH LOFTY TOWERS SOARING ABOVE LIGHTLESS, PERILOUS UNDERLEVELS. ONCE THE CAPITAL OF THE REPUBLIC AND THE EMPIRE, IT'S BELIEVED TO BE THE BIRTHPLACE OF HUMANITY. SADLY, AFTER THE FALL OF THE EMPIRE, THE GLITTERING WORLD FELL UNDER THE CONTROL OF CRIMINAL SYNDICATES. GANGS NOW PROWL EVEN RESPECTABLE DISTRICTS, AND SAFETY IS RESERVED FOR THOSE WHO CAN AFFORD ARMED GUARDS AND DROID PROTECTORS. TOURISM HAS ALL BUT DISAPPEARED, AND CORUSCANT HAS BECOME A SYMBOL NOT OF GALACTIC POSSIBILITIES, BUT OF THE CURRENT ERA'S DISTURBING REALITIES.

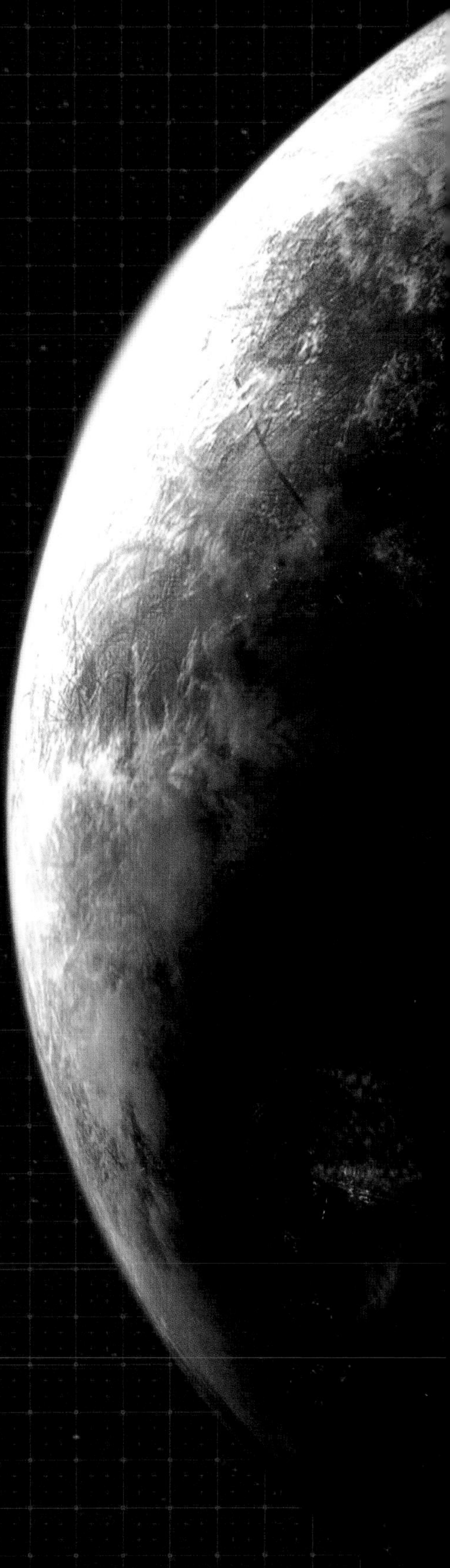

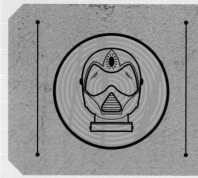

DK-RA-43'S COMMENT

Coruscant's descent into lawlessness is one of the greatest tragedies of our age. What a rich history! To walk the promenade of the Galaxies Opera House! Fly by the towers of the Verity District! This planet – this glorious, glittering planet – is the ultimate in galactic culture! Oh, for better days when civilized beings will visit once again!

OVERVIEW

FEDERAL DISTRICT • IMPERIAL PALACE • MONUMENT PLAZA • 500 REPUBLICA • VERITY DISTRICT
USCRU DISTRICT • GALAXIES OPERA HOUSE • COCO TOWN • THE WORKS

HISTORY

The long-time galactic capital and center of culture and power, Coruscant has suffered gravely since the Empire's fall, with criminal gangs fighting a bloody war for control of its districts.

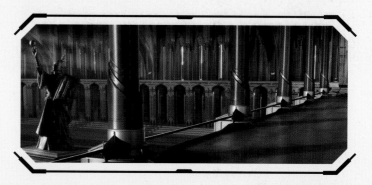

VEHICLE

CORUSCANT AIR TAXI

Offworlders see the skylanes of Coruscant as a terrifying river of airspeeders, swoops, skybuses, and transports, but the traffic actually flows surprisingly well for a planet with a trillion residents. Traffic-control networks take command of vehicles in skylanes, with air taxis — flown by famously gruff, fearless air-jockeys — free to take more direct routes.

GALAXIES OPERA HOUSE

Two generations ago, the Senate Building was the seat of political power, the Jedi Temple promised galactic peace, and the Galaxies Opera House was the pinnacle of culture. But the Imperial Senate was disbanded and the New Republic Senate operated elsewhere. Only the Opera House remains, a symbol of hope that Coruscant will rise again.

SUPPORT
THE GALAXIES
OPERA
HOUSE

SPECIES/CREATURES

HUMANS

Coruscant has long been claimed as the cradle world from which humanity spread to dominate the galaxy. Scientists disagree about whether that's true, but scientific controversies aside, Coruscant is clearly the center of human culture. Even given its current woes, Coruscant inspires humans stuck on backwater planets to dream of limitless possibilities and dizzying luxuries.

KOUHUNS

These small, deadly arthropods are native to Indoumodo, and kill their prey with a fast-acting nerve toxin. They are a favored tool of assassins, as they can evade security and are extremely difficult to trace back to their users. Kouhuns used in assassinations are starved to make them vicious, but those employing them must beware – a single miscalculation and the kouhun will happily sink its fangs into the assassin instead of the target. Zam Wesell used a pair of kouhuns to target Padmé Amidala, Naboo's senator.

HISTORY

THE GALACTIC CONCORDANCE

After Endor, Grand Vizier Mas Amedda held power on Coruscant, but the warlord Gallius Rax saw no future for the capital, placing Amedda under house arrest in the Imperial Palace. Coruscant was rocked by war between Imperial factions, with crime syndicates rushing to fill the power vacuum. Amedda finally escaped and signed the Galactic Concordance with the New Republic, ending the Galactic Civil War.

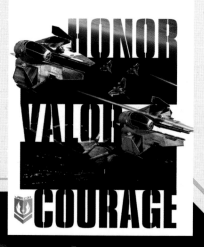

VEHICLES

JEDI INTERCEPTOR

Formally known as the Eta-2 *Actis*-class interceptor, the Jedi interceptor was designed for pilots with Force-aided reflexes, emphasizing speed and agility and stripping away sensors, shields and bulky instrument packages. Obi-Wan Kenobi and Anakin Skywalker piloted Jedi interceptors above Coruscant, racing between dueling battleships to rescue Supreme Chancellor Palpatine from General Grievous' ship.

DROID

CAM DROIDS

For millennia, the Senate was a galactic institution, conducting its business in a huge chamber in the Federal District. Cam droids were ever-present, swooping around senators' platforms and recording their words and images for broadcast across the galaxy. Wise senators played to their fellow politicians but also to those watching remotely.

HOLOSCANNER

WEAPON

SENATE GUARD RIFLE

Clad in blue robes and crested helmets, the Senate Guard protected the Chancellor and the Senate with Mk. II Paladin rifles.

MAS AMEDDA

A Chagrian politician from Champala, Mas Amedda had a gift for political survival. He served Chancellor Valorum, transferred his loyalties to the ascendant Chancellor Palpatine, whom he also served, and survived to make peace with the New Republic and lead Coruscant's postwar government.

DEXTER JETTSTER

Coruscant attracted not just politicians but scientists, artists, and entrepreneurs with ambitions big and small. The four-armed Besalisk Dexter Jettster ran a diner in Coco Town for decades, serving comfort food and becoming a valuable intelligence source for his many friends, among them the Jedi Knight Obi-Wan Kenobi.

ROGUES' GALLERY

GENERAL GRIEVOUS

In the final days of the Clone Wars, the Separatist warlord General Grievous launched a daring raid on Coruscant with a task force, kidnapping Supreme Chancellor Palpatine. The Jedi thwarted the kidnapping, but falling debris from the orbital battle left scars that still marred the cityscape decades later. Obi-Wan Kenobi eventually hunted down and killed Grievous on the planet Utapau.

ZAM WESELL

A shapeshifting Clawdite assassin, Zam Wesell made a fatal error when she agreed to accept a risky assignment from the bounty hunter Jango Fett. Her attempt to assassinate Naboo's Senator Amidala failed, and two Jedi captured her. Before they could interrogate Zam, Fett ended her career with a saberdart dipped in poison.

362

JAKKU

PLANETARY DATA

SECTOR: None

SYSTEM: Jakku

TYPE: Terrestrial

CLIMATE: Hot and arid

DIAMETER: 6,400 km

TERRAIN: Desert, badlands

ROTATION PERIOD: 27 standard hours

ORBITAL PERIOD: 362 local rotations

SENTIENT SPECIES: Teedos

POPULATION: Unknown

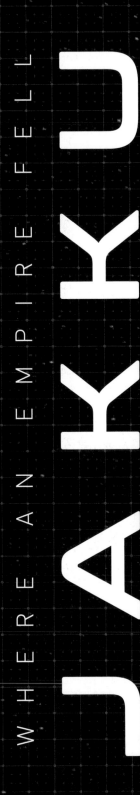

WHERE AN EMPIRE FELL

JAKKU

A DESERT PLANET ON THE EDGE
OF THE GALACTIC FRONTIER,
JAKKU IS NOTABLE AS THE SITE
OF THE BATTLE THAT ENDED
THE GALACTIC CIVIL WAR. ITS
SAND SEAS AND BADLANDS
ARE LITTERED WITH WRECKED
WARSHIPS, MANY OF THEM
FOUND IN AN EERIE STRETCH
OF DESERT KNOWN AS "THE
GRAVEYARD OF SHIPS." THIS
BLEAK AREA IS JAKKU'S ONLY
SOURCE OF COMMERCE.
SCAVENGERS SEARCH THESE
WRECKS FOR ANYTHING THEY
CAN SALVAGE, EKING OUT A
LIVING AND DREAMING OF
ESCAPING TO A BETTER LIFE.
JAKKU'S INHABITANTS TRADE
NOT ONLY SALVAGE BUT ALSO
RUMORS ABOUT GREAT SECRETS
BURIED BENEATH THE SAND.
BUT YOU CAN'T EAT STORIES,
AND FEW ON JAKKU EVER FIND
ANYTHING EXCEPT HARDSHIP,
DISAPPOINTMENT, AND
LONELINESS.

OVERVIEW

NIIMA OUTPOST • CARBON RIDGE • GRAVEYARD OF SHIPS • THE SINKING FIELDS • GOAZON BADLANDS
PLAINTIVE HAND PLATEAU • BLOWBACK TOWN • CRATERTOWN

HISTORY

An obscure frontier world, Jakku was the site of the final battle between the New Republic and what remained of the Empire. The orbital slugging match left the planet's deserts littered with wreckage, which desperate scavengers have picked over ever since.

ᗡᐯᑎᑭᗅᐯᑎ ᒐᗋ ᒐᐯᗋᑌᑌᑌ

DK-RA-43'S COMMENT

Jakku is a lawless place with zero of interest except the Graveyard of Ships, and that is an extremely dangerous place! Its perils include (while not being limited to) radiation, toxic chemicals, and undetonated ordnance, and the scavengers who make their living salvaging parts from the battlefield are thieves and murderers. Mark my words, this visit will not end well!

VEHICLES

IMPERIAL STAR DESTROYER

The backbone of the Imperial Navy, these massive warships packed tremendous firepower and carried a full wing of TIE fighters, as well as troops and vehicles sufficient to crush rebel planets. They served not only as engines of military might but also as psychological weapons, with their distinctive dagger shape striking terror in the Empire's enemies.

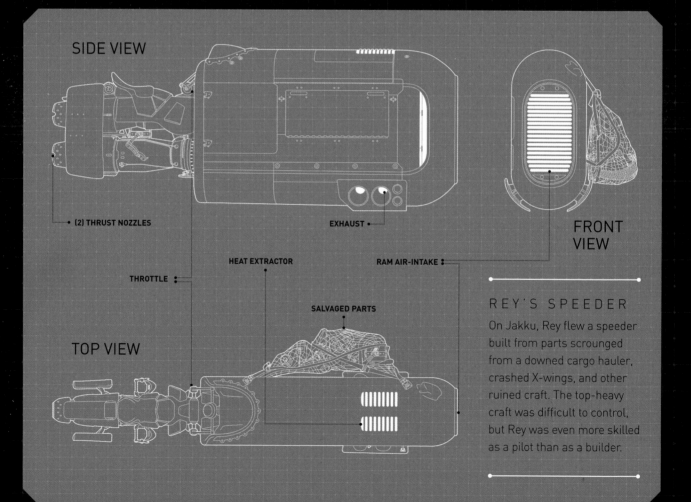

SIDE VIEW

• (2) THRUST NOZZLES

EXHAUST •

FRONT VIEW

HEAT EXTRACTOR

THROTTLE •

RAM AIR-INTAKE •

SALVAGED PARTS

TOP VIEW

REY'S SPEEDER

On Jakku, Rey flew a speeder built from parts scrounged from a downed cargo hauler, crashed X-wings, and other ruined craft. The top-heavy craft was difficult to control, but Rey was even more skilled as a pilot than as a builder.

CREATURES/SPECIES

STEELPECKERS/ NIGHTWATCHER WORMS

Despite its harsh conditions, Jakku has abundant life. Steelpeckers hunt for metal they can devour, gnaw-jaws emerge at night to hunt prey, and skittermice hide in their burrows. Jakku's most feared lifeform is the nightwatcher worm, however. It can top 20 meters in length. These predators swim through the sands, emerging when they sense surface vibrations.

HOLOSCANNER

TEEDOS

Diminutive humanoids, Teedos prowl the wastes of Jakku, often riding cybernetically altered luggabeasts. Fiercely territorial, they are rumored to have a strange form of telepathic awareness, with one Teedo often knowing of events to befall another. They make no distinction between individuals: All Teedos are known as Teedo. Biologists argue over whether they are native to Jakku or arrived at some point in the distant past.

THE TIDES OF HISTORY

As soon as warships plummeted from orbit to crash in the sands of Jakku, scavengers began picking over the wreckage for weapons, gear, fuel, and machinery. A generation after the Battle of Jakku, scavenging remains the planet's only real industry, with the shifting sands constantly revealing new wrecks. Jakku's scavengers jealously guard their finds with surplus and improvised weapons, hauling away intact components to clean at Niima Outpost's washing stations and trade for food or other scarce supplies.

THE GRAVEYARD OF SHIPS

Jakku's famous Graveyard of Ships is its only real attraction, with the giant wrecks casting forlorn shadows over the austere landscape. Scavengers and other roustabouts can be persuaded to play tour guide, but the price is steep, safety isn't assured, and all salvage belongs to the scavenger. Travelers should also take note that Jakku's towns have few services expected on more civilized worlds, but many thieves and grifters hoping to find victims.

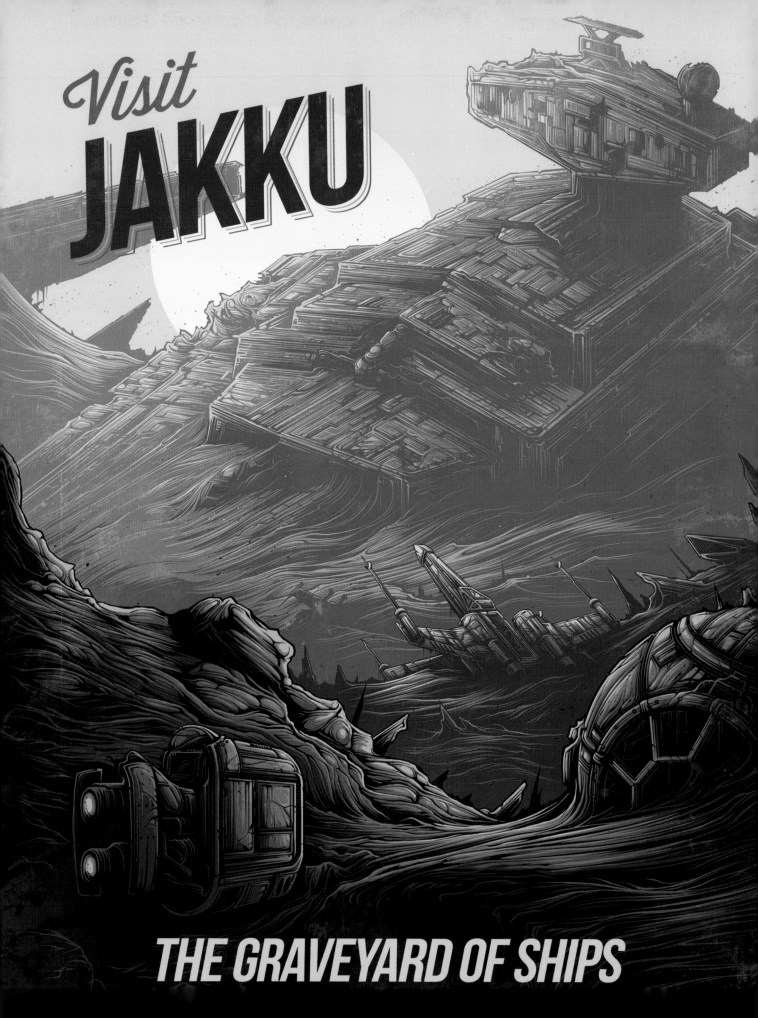

PERSONS OF INTEREST

FINN

FN-2187 was raised by the First Order, fed a steady diet of propaganda and trained as a stormtrooper. But Finn (as Poe Dameron renamed him) rejected his brainwashing and defected, helping Dameron escape and playing a key role in the raid that destroyed Starkiller Base. He then had to decide whether to join the Resistance or seek a peaceful life away from the horrors of war.

REY

A Jakku scavenger of mysterious origins, Rey became a hero of the Resistance, leading the mission to find Luke Skywalker and persuade him to leave his lonely exile. In encountering Skywalker, she began to unlock her vast potential with the Force, offering a new hope to a galaxy threatened by the military might of the resurgent First Order.

LOR SAN TEKKA

An adherent of the Church of the Force and a tireless explorer, Lor San Tekka restored much knowledge of the Jedi that had been erased by the Empire. Knowing he was in his final years, San Tekka retired to Jakku, but his retirement was anything but peaceful; the Resistance and the First Order both sought him as the key to finding the vanished Luke Skywalker.

UNKAR PLUTT

A Crolute from the waterworld Crul, Unkar Plutt wound up on Jakku – about the least hospitable place for his species – after a series of failed business deals, settling in as the boss of Niima Outpost and its scavengers. He was briefly the owner of the *Millennium Falcon*, which he acquired from the Irving Boys.

THE SLICE

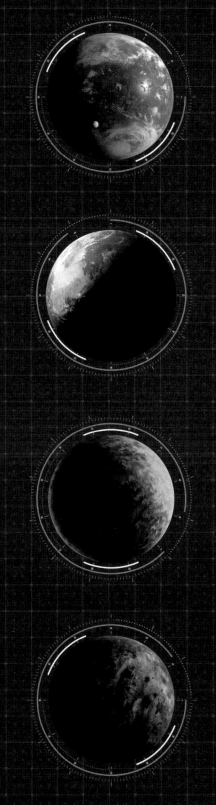

KASHYYYK

Kashyyyk is a green planet featuring a series of vertical ecosystems, all dependent on its massive, kilometers-high wroshyr trees. The Wookiees dwell in the sunny treetops, while predators prowl the dangerous darkness around the wroshyrs' great roots.

TATOOINE

A desert planet orbiting twin suns, Tatooine has long been ruled by the Hutts, who use it as a trading post for illicit goods smuggled across the Outer Rim. Despite its harsh climate, Tatooine is rich in life adapted for surviving in harmony with the rhythms of the desert.

GEONOSIS

A rugged world of mesas and badlands, Geonosis was once the homeworld of the Geonosians, an insect species known as clever designers and engineers. The Empire built the first Death Star at Geonosis, and sterilized the planet to keep this secret.

KESSEL

A barren world located at the heart of a treacherous tangle of black holes and other hazards, Kessel is the center of the galactic trade in spice and coaxium. Navigating the famed Kessel Run is a rite of passage for those seeking to prove their mettle as pilots.

NEW TERRITORIES

- Dantooine
- Cantonica
- Yavin
- Felucia
- Dathomir
- Mon Cala
- Ithor
- Lothal
- Ord Mantell
- Ilum
- Mandalore

HYDIAN WAY

PERLEMIAN TRADE ROUTE

CHISS ASCENDENCY
- Csilla
- Jedha

THE INTERIOR

- Alderaan
- Coruscant

THE SLICE

- KASHYYYK
- KESSEL
- Toydaria
- Nal Hutta

HUTT SPACE

UNKNOWN REGIONS

- Ahch-To
- Jakku
- Corellia
- Hosnian Prime

SPINE

CORELLIAN RUN

BOTHAN SPACE
- Bothawui

- Scarif

- Batuu
- Takodana

CORELLIAN TRADE

- Rodia
- TATOOINE
- GEONOSIS

- Endor

- Naboo
- Crait
- Sullust
- D'Qar

WESTERN REACHES

- Bespin
- Hoth
- Mustafar
- Dagobah
- Utapau

RIMMA TRADE ROUTE

TRAILING SECTORS

381

KASHYYYK

PLANETARY DATA

SECTOR: Mytaranor

TYPE: Terrestrial

CLIMATE: Temperate and moist

DIAMETER: 12,765 km

TERRAIN: Forests

ROTATION PERIOD: 26 standard hours

ORBITAL PERIOD: 381 local rotations

SENTIENT SPECIES: Wookiees

POPULATION: 56 million

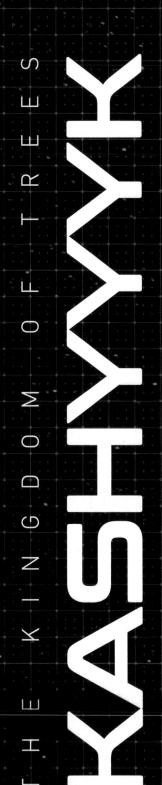

KASHYYYK

A GREEN WORLD OF MASSIVE TREES, KASHYYYK IS HOME TO THE WOOKIEES, BRAVE WARRIORS WHO ENDURED DECADES AS FORCED LABOR FOR BOTH IMPERIAL GOVERNORS AND GALACTIC CRIME GANGS. THE PLANET BEARS THE SCARS OF OCCUPATION AND WAR, BUT YEARS OF RELATIVE PEACE ARE ALLOWING THE FORESTS TO HEAL. VISITORS TO KASHYYYK WILL DISCOVER A WILD WORLD OF VARIED ECOSYSTEMS: THE TOPS OF THE WROSHYR TREES ARE BREEZY AND SUNNY, BUT THE WORLD AT THEIR ROOTS IS DARK AND DANGEROUS.

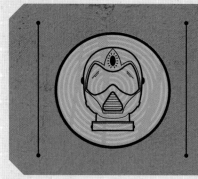

DK-RA-43'S COMMENT

"Kashyyyk's lofty wroshyr forests are a galactic treasure, and the Wookiees' commitment to living in harmony with nature is an admirable belief that other species could learn from. But this is one planet where I most definitely recommend sticking close to your guide! Descend below the sunny treetops and you soon find yourself in a shadowy realm prowled by vicious predators. Only the bravest Wookiees dare enter the lightless world of the Kashyyyk depths."

OVERVIEW

KACHIRHO • WAWAATT ARCHIPELAGO • RWOOKRRORRO

HISTORY

The Empire brutally exploited Kashyyyk, reclassifying it as Territory G5-623, forcing Wookiees to work as conscript labour, and despoiling its forests. The planet was the site of a key battle at the end of the Clone Wars and was liberated by the New Republic soon after the Battle of Endor.

CATAMARAN

While Wookiees may appear primitive, they are superb builders, marrying advanced technology with lovingly crafted wood and other natural resources. Wookiee catamarans are speedy, manoeuvrable watercraft that use twin repulsorlift engines to race across Kashyyyk's bays and bayous at breakneck speed.

PECIES

OOKIEES

shyyyk's Wookiees are powerful, aggy bipeds. Though they look fierce, ve short tempers, and can let loose h terrifying bellows, Wookiees are cually peace-loving and loyal. Many d during the Imperial occupation, en against their will, but a number ve now returned to their treetop mes, eager to rebuild their planet.

KACHIRHO

The capital of Kashyyyk, Kachirho sprawls along the shoreline of the tropica Wawaatt Archipelago. Its massive wroshyr trees still bear the scars of battles during the Clone Wars, when Separatist droids fought to seize the capita from clone troopers and Wookiee defenders, and the damage left by Imperia occupation. The planet has healed quickly, however, and tourists now seek ou Kachirho's platforms, enjoying the warm breezes, fresh air and sense of peace o a planet that all but thrums with the energies of inexhaustible life.

PERSONS OF INTEREST

CHEWBACCA

A legendary smuggler and rebel hero, Chewbacca fought in the Clone Wars on his homeworld, then served alongside his beloved friend Han Solo as first mate of the *Millennium Falcon*. His exploits at Yavin, Hoth, Endor, Starkiller Base, and Crait made the Wookiee an enduring symbol in the fight for freedom.

YODA

The Jedi Grandmaster in the last days of the Republic, Yoda defended Kashyyyk against Separatist attackers, and was on the forest planet when Order 66 came and the clone troopers rose up against their Jedi generals. He was one of the few survivors of the purge, escaping Republic troops with the help of the Wookiees.

LUMINARA UNDULI

A wise Mirialan Jedi Master, Luminara Unduli fought in both Battles of Geonosis and on Kashyyyk. She survived Order 66 but was arrested by Imperial agents and executed. She was master to Barriss Offee and a mentor for Ahsoka Tano and Caleb Dume, later known as the rebel hero Kanan Jarrus.

304

TATOOINE

PLANETARY DATA

SECTOR: Arkanis

SYSTEM: Tatooine

TYPE: Terrestrial

CLIMATE: Hot and arid

DIAMETER: 10,465 km

TERRAIN: Desert

ROTATION PERIOD: 23 standard days

ORBITAL PERIOD: 304 local rotations

SENTIENT SPECIES: Tusken Raiders, Jawas

POPULATION: 1.1 million

TATOOINE

A BLEAK, DRY DESERT WORLD BAKED BY TWIN SUNS, TATOOINE HAS LONG BEEN A POPULAR DESTINATION FOR SHADY CHARACTERS INCLUDING SMUGGLERS, GAMBLERS, AND FUGITIVES FROM JUSTICE. THOUGH FAR FROM THE GALAXY'S BRIGHT CENTER, TATOOINE HAS SHAPED GALACTIC HISTORY: IT'S THE HOMEWORLD OF ALLIANCE HERO LUKE SKYWALKER AND WAS THE HEADQUARTERS FOR CRIMEBOSS JABBA THE HUTT. TATOOINE'S LAWLESS REPUTATION MAKES IT A DRAW FOR PODRACING FANS AND TOURISTS WITH AN APPRECIATION FOR THE WILDER SIDE OF LIFE.

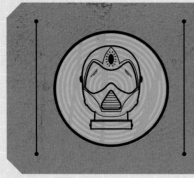

DK-RA-43'S COMMENT

"Tatooine? This is one of the more baffling requests I've received. The desert landscapes of Venerable Stirta are far more scenic, Palmatian II offers gambling without the likelihood of winding up in a shock collar or a shallow grave, and my database includes 364,988 tourist destinations not controlled by criminal enterprises. But my purpose is to serve. If only my programming modules included more information about the fascinating subject of moisture farming."

OVERVIEW

BEGGAR'S CANYON • DUNE SEA • GREAT CHOTT SALT FLAT • GREAT MESRA PLATEAU • GREAT PIT OF CARKOON • JABBA'S PALACE • JUNDLAND CHASM • MOS EISLEY • MUSHROOM MESA • MOS ESPA

HISTORY

A failed mining colony, Tatooine is home to hardy moisture farmers, but its real economic value is as a smuggling hub located at a juncture of Outer Rim hyperspace routes. Hutt crime families have controlled Tatooine for many decades and continue to operate with little regard for galactic law.

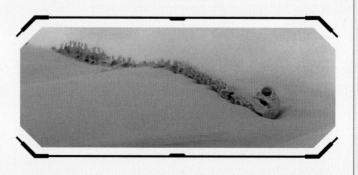

SPECIES

TUSKEN RAIDERS

Native Tatooine species include banthas, rontos, eopies, dewbacks, and the legendary krayt dragons. Its most dangerous inhabitants are the Tusken Raiders, belligerent nomads who consider the planet's water sacred. Tuskens raid frontier settlements, carrying away unlucky moisture farmers for ritual torture and sacrifice.

JAWAS

Jawas hide their bodies behind tattered rags and hoods. They scour Tatooine's dunes and badlands in their mobile sandcrawlers, searching for scrap metal and abandoned droids. If you're hoping for a bargain from Jawa traders, think again; many of their wares turn out to be stolen, and Jawa repairs often break down after the scavengers' sandcrawler has trundled out of sight over the next dune.

WEAPONS

ION BLASTER

Jawas use ion blasters crafted from scavenged parts to subdue droids or stun organic beings.

GADERFFII STICK

Also known as gaffi sticks, these Tusken war clubs are made from metal scrounged from desert wrecks.

TECHNOLOGY

MOISTURE VAPORATOR

Vaporators draw water from the air, collecting it for storage or reuse in hydroponic farming. Moisture farmers rely on these machines for their livelihood

Welcome To MOS EISLEY

Home of The Famous Chalmun's Cantina

WATERING HOLE: MOS EISLEY CANTINA

Oh, the stories they can tell in this Mos Eisley dive, used for decades as a clubhouse by pilots of all species. We'd say bring a translator droid, but Chalmun's policy is NO DROIDS ALLOWED. Stay out of the shadowy back alcoves and beware of locals starting fights. While Figrin D'an and the Modal Nodes have moved on, house bands still play "Mad About Me," "Dune Sea Special," and other hits.

MOS ESPA ARENA
PODRACING
ON TATOOINE

Love speed and the crackle of engine ions? Comfortable with a non-zero chance you'll be torn to ribbons by a hurtling engine? Then podracing's your sport! Rarely seen in the central systems due to pesky safety regulations, it thrives in the Outer Rim. Tatooine has several arenas, but true fans swap tips about wildcat races held in the desert. Expect powerful machines, vicious tactics, and spectacular crashes. Sitting next to an old-timer? Ask about Anakin Skywalker's legendary victory at

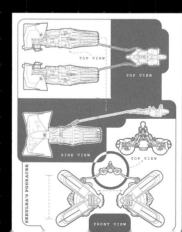

TOP VIEW

TOP VIEW

SIDE VIEW

TOP VIEW

SEBULBA'S PODRACER

FRONT VIEW

JABBA'S PALACE

Located on the fringes of the Northern Dune Sea, Jabba the Hutt's palace is an ancient labyrinth containing many secrets. Originally home to the B'omarr Order's monks, it served Jabba for years as a base of operations, with the Hutt conducting business from a throne room thronged with grifters, killers, and other galactic refuse. Jabba fed those who displeased him to a rancor kept chained below this chamber, with particularly unlucky prisoners cast into the Great Pit of Carkoon, where they were devoured by a tentacled Sarlacc.

THE *KHETANNA*

Ubrikkian artisans custom-built this sail barge for Jabba the Hutt's use as a floating palace, complete with a throne room, private lounges, and a well-appointed kitchen. Jabba used the *Khetanna* for meetings in the Dune Sea and as a viewing platform for the execution of prisoners at the Great Pit of Carkoon. Luke Skywalker and his rebel friends destroyed the barge at the end of their mission to rescue Han Solo, killing the Hutt and throwing the Outer Rim's criminal underworld into chaos.

ROGUES' GALLERY
JABBA THE HUTT

A wily and ruthless crime boss, Jabba the Hutt ruled a sprawling Outer Rim criminal empire from his palace in Tatooine's Dune Sea, supervising a network of smugglers, pirates, slavers, and guns for hire. The Hutt met his end shortly before the Empire's fall, as Leia Organa strangled him with the chain he'd used to imprison her.

TWIN SUN STARLINES

TAT
TATOOINE
A WRETCHED HIVE OF SCUM & VILLAINY

YT-1300/11-38

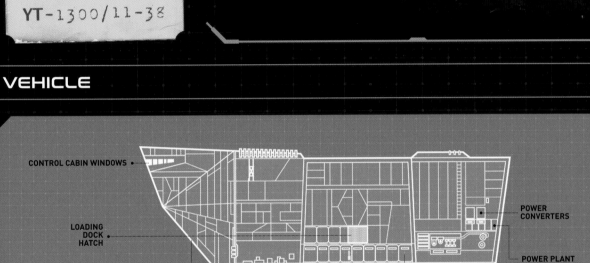

VEHICLE

SIDE VIEW

- CONTROL CABIN WINDOWS
- LOADING DOCK HATCH
- RETRACTABLE FRONT HATCH
- MAIN ACCESS HATCH
- MAGNETIC SUCTION TUBE
- LOWER INSPECTION HATCH (STAIRWAY RETRACTED)
- INSPECTION PANELS
- POWER CONVERTERS
- POWER PLANT
- HEAVY-DUTY TREAD ASSEMBLY (8)

FRONT VIEW

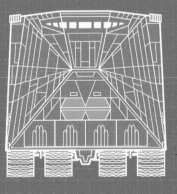

SANDCRAWLER

Originally built for Tatooine's brief-lived mineral boom, sandcrawlers are giant treaded vehicles used by native Jawas as mobile foundries, trading posts, repair bays, and homes. Jawa clans follow traditional routes across the desert, scavenging metal for their own use or for resale to the planet's settlers.

CREATURES

SARLACC
(GREAT PIT OF CARKOON)

Sarlaccs dwell in pits in Tatooine's Dune Sea, ensnaring prey with tentacles radiating from their toothy maws. Jabba the Hutt enjoyed executing prisoners by feeding them to the Great Pit of Carkoon's resident Sarlacc. Questions about this strange predator's natural lifespan, possible sentience, and origin remain hotly contested.

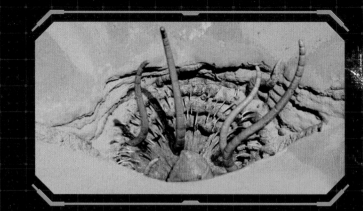

BANTHA

Banthas are common on many worlds, and bred for their meat, wool, hides, and milk. Tatooine's Tusken Raiders have a deep connection with banthas, which they ride into battle. Young Tuskens form close bonds with their banthas, and if a rider dies, his or her mount will typically refuse to eat and soon die as well.

HOLOSCANNER

DEWBACK

These plodding but hardy reptiles are Tatooine's most reliable beasts of burden, less temperamental as mounts than jerbas, rontos, or banthas. Dewbacks are cold-blooded and become sluggish at night. They huddle together for warmth and lick the accumulated dew off each other's backs in the morning.

PERSON OF INTEREST

LUKE SKYWALKER

Before he became legendary as destroyer of the Death Star and preserver of the Jedi Order, Luke Skywalker was a farm boy living near the dusty town of Anchorhead, stuck with endless chores and the nickname Wormie. His unlikely story has given hope to restless youths on many galactic worlds.

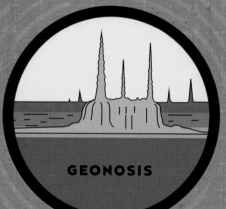

GEONOSIS

PLANETARY DATA

SECTOR: Arkanis

TYPE: Terrestrial

CLIMATE: Arid

DIAMETER: 11,370 km

TERRAIN: Rocks, desert

ROTATION PERIOD: 30 standard hours

ORBITAL PERIOD: 256 local rotations

SENTIENT SPECIES: None (formerly Geonosians)

POPULATION: None

SECTION TWO

GEONOSIS

ONCE INTRODUCED TO GALACTIC TECHNOLOGY, THIS HARSH, ARID WORLD'S INSECTILE INHABITANTS PROVED ADEPT AT DROID PRODUCTION AND DISMISSIVE OF REPUBLIC REGULATIONS AND LAWS. THE GEONOSIAN HIVES BUILT ARMIES OF BATTLE DROIDS FOR THE TRADE FEDERATION, THEN SUPPLIED WAR MATÉRIEL TO THE SEPARATISTS. THE CLONE WARS BEGAN WITH A JEDI RESCUE MISSION TO GEONOSIS BACKED BY CLONE TROOPERS FROM KAMINO; LATER, AN INVASION WAS REQUIRED TO DISRUPT THE FLOW OF GEONOSIAN DROID SOLDIERS. THE EMPIRE BUILT THE FIRST DEATH STAR ABOVE GEONOSIS, THEN STERILIZED THE PLANET AS A RUTHLESS SECURITY PRECAUTION.

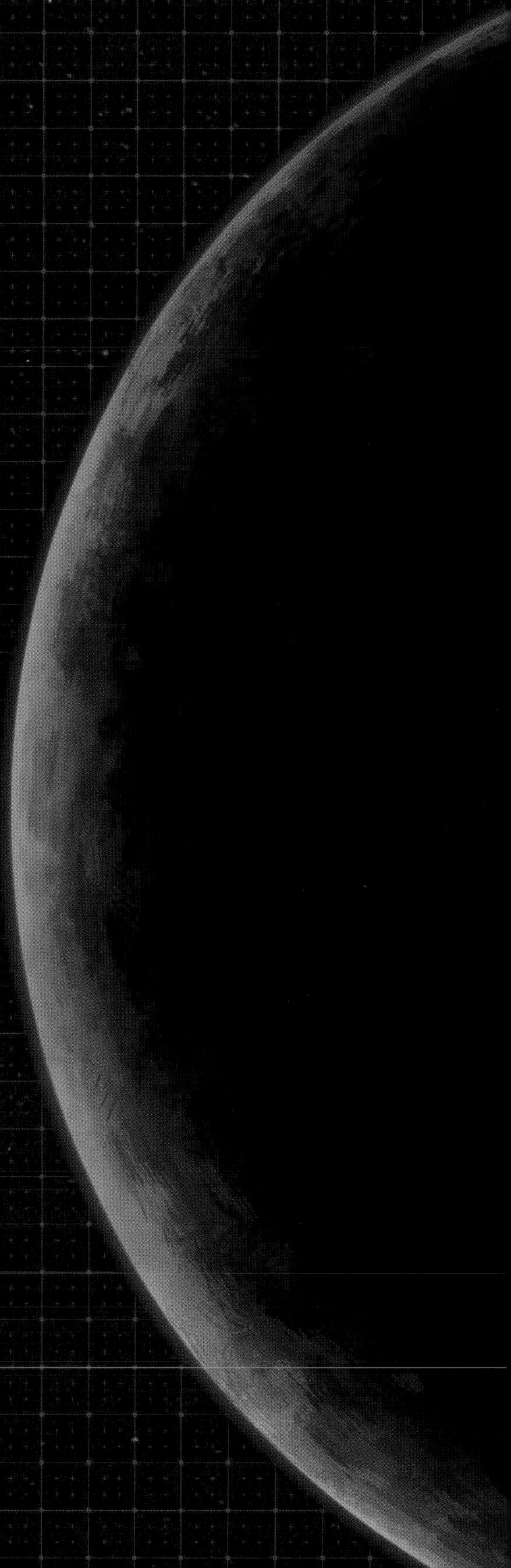

OVERVIEW

DROID FACTORY • EXECUTION ARENA •
PROGATE TEMPLE • KORAKANNI MOUND

HISTORY

Geonosians were geniuses at designing
and producing machines, skills they
contributed to the Separatist cause during
the Clone Wars before being forced to
work for the Empire.

DK-RA-43'S COMMENT

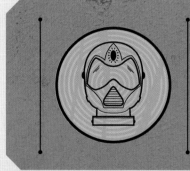

"Another inhospitable planet, and this one doesn't even have inhabitants!
Still, from what my databanks have recorded about Geonosians, that's
no loss; all that clattering and chittering would make me short-circuit.
When we decide to visit anyway, make sure to take a properly rated
breath mask. And I'll need an oil bath – in premium lubricants, this time
– to ensure I don't bring back any lethal contaminants."

CREATURE

ORRAY

Sturdy quadrupeds, orrays were bred and raised by Geonosians as mounts and beasts of burden. Wild orrays have stingers on their whip-like tails, which Geonosians amputated for safety and to make the creatures more docile. These creatures are now believed to be extinct.

SPECIES

GEONOSIAN

Geonosian society was segregated into rigid castes, with worker and soldier drones expected to toil endlessly for the upper castes of their towering hive complexes. Social unrest was rare but explosive, so hive nobles channelled it into gladiatorial spectacles and wars with rival colonies. During the Clone Wars, the Republic discovered that rumours about a higher caste were true; the hives answered to queens who ruled from subterranean brood chambers.

VEHICLE

SOLAR SAILER

The Geonosian hives built droids and vehicles for wealthy individuals as well as galactic corporations and planetary governments. One of their most elegant creations was an interstellar sloop designed by Poggle the Lesser as a gift for Count Dooku. The craft used a huge solar sail of ancient design to travel along the galaxy's spacelanes.

DROIDS

B1 BATTLE DROID

The Trade Federation used an army of B1s directed by a Droid Control Ship to invade and occupy Naboo. Billions of these Geonosian-designed "clankers" then saw service in the Clone Wars. B1s were cheaply made and largely ineffective in combat, but their sheer numbers allowed them to overwhelm enemies.

HOLOSCANNER

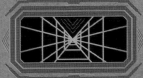

DEATH STAR

An armored battle station the size of a small moon, the Death Star was built around
a superlaser dish powerful enough to destroy a planet. The project was overseen by
the Empire above Geonosis using forced Geonosian labor, with access to the planet
restricted to a small cadre of Imperial engineers and military leaders.

The **DEATH STAR**

IMPERIAL BATTLESTATION

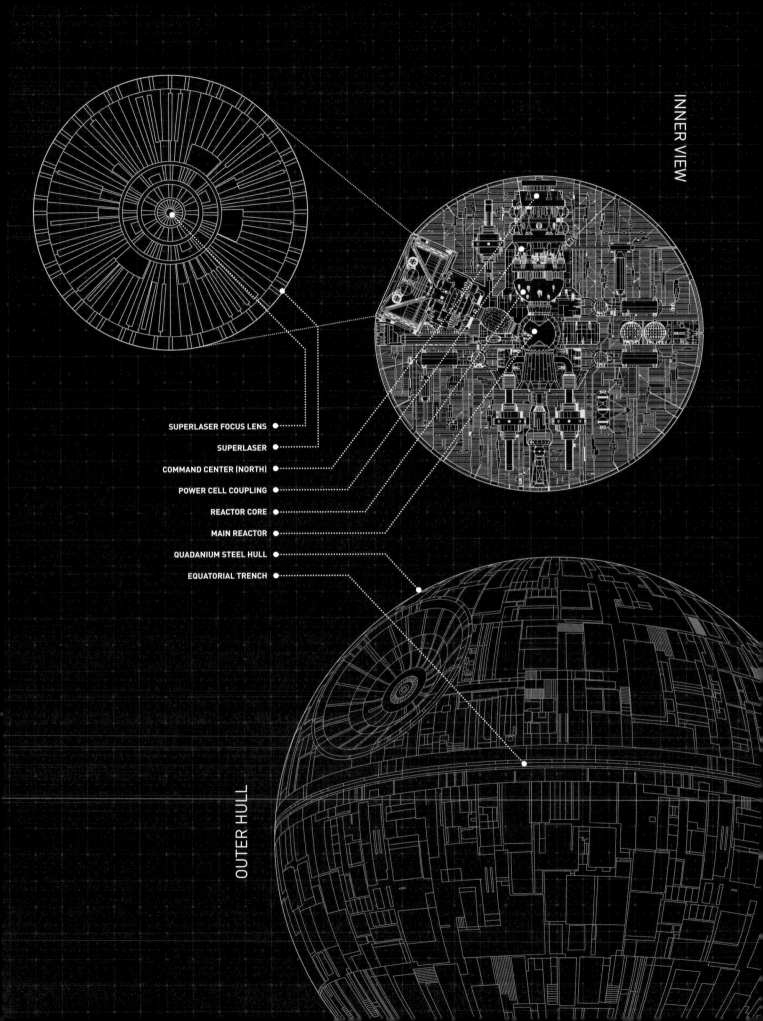

SUPERLASER FOCUS LENS

SUPERLASER

COMMAND CENTER (NORTH)

POWER CELL COUPLING

REACTOR CORE

MAIN REACTOR

QUADANIUM STEEL HULL

EQUATORIAL TRENCH

OUTER HULL

HOLOSCANNER

SURVIVE AN ATTACK
OF BATTLE DROIDS

PERSONS OF INTEREST

SAW GERRERA

Saw Gerrera fought the Separatists as a youth on Onderon, then became a partisan known for his ruthless tactics in battling the Empire. Saw became obsessed with rumours that the Empire was building a planet-killer, a quest that led him to the lifeless wastes of Geonosis in search of answers.

CLONE TROOPER

With the Separatists preparing for war, the Jedi discovered Kamino's cloners had grown an army of soldiers trained from birth to serve the Republic. Yoda led these clone troopers to Geonosis, marking the first battle of the Clone Wars and the beginning of an ill-fated partnership between Jedi and clones.

ROGUES' GALLERY

POGGLE THE LESSER

The leader of the Stalgasin Hive, Poggle the Lesser was a rare Geonosian who rose to power from his hive's lower castes, an ascension that owed much to secret financial help from mysterious backers. He was captured by the Republic, escaped custody, and died on Mustafar at the end of the Clone Wars.

COUNT DOOKU

The charismatic political leader of the Confederacy of Independent Systems, Count Dooku was one of the few Jedi Masters to leave the Order, and his fiery speeches against Republic corruption swayed many systems to the Separatist cause. His duties brought him to many Separatist worlds, including Geonosis and its droid foundries.

KESSEL

PLANETARY DATA

SECTOR: Kessel

TYPE: Terrestrial

CLIMATE: Hot

DIAMETER: 7,200 km

TERRAIN: Mountains, badlands, forest

ROTATION PERIOD: 12 standard hours

ORBITAL PERIOD: 322 local rotations

SENTIENT SPECIES: None

POPULATION: 10,000

SECTION TWO

KESSEL

WHETHER YOU'RE A PRISONER OR A DROID, A PRISON SENTENCE ON KESSEL IS TANTAMOUNT TO A DEATH SENTENCE. FOR GENERATIONS, LUCKLESS LABORERS TOILED IN THE GRIM PLANET'S MINES, BREAKING UP KESSELSTONE TO EXTRACT SPICE AND COAXIUM. THE CRIMINAL PYKE SYNDICATE STRUCK A DEAL WITH KESSEL'S KING YARUBA TO MINE HALF THE PLANET, WITH THE EMPIRE OFFERING A STEADY SUPPLY OF SLAVE LABOR, INCLUDING BOTH COMMON CRIMINALS AND POLITICAL UNDESIRABLES. KESSEL LIES AMID A TANGLE OF NAVIGATIONAL HAZARDS; FOR A HOT PILOT WITH A FAST SHIP, THERE'S NO TRUER TEST OF NERVE AND SKILL THAN MAKING THE PERILOUS KESSEL RUN AWAY FROM THE WRETCHED PLANET.

OVERVIEW

KESSEL CITY • SPICE MINES

HISTORY

Kessel's spice mines have been infamous for centuries. They produce spice, which is easily converted into a powerful narcotic, and coaxium, a volatile fuel critical for hyperspace travel.

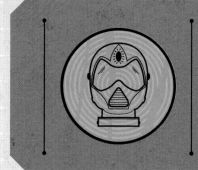

DK-RA-43'S COMMENT

"You must be joking! I had thought that I'd at least be spared spending precious processor cycles to consider this horrible place. Slave labor, toxins, and the very real possibility of dying in some horrible spaceflight accident? Why, it's a mystery that Kessel isn't considered the garden spot of the galaxy! Perhaps I should collect these dossiers as *A Wretched Travelogue of Awful Planets That No Sane Being Should Visit*."

Native to Oba Diah, the Pykes have tapered skulls and bright eyes. As the Republic crumbled, the Pyke Syndicate gained control of spice production on Kessel, providing a flow of credits for the gang's other criminal enterprises. Pyke operatives dreaded being posted to the spice world, however, as they were allergic to pollutants in its air – a momentary reminder of the worse fate facing the laborers being worked to their deaths in the cramped tunnels below.

ROGUES' GALLERY

QUAY TOLSITE

Before the Battle of Yavin, Quay Tolsite served as director of the Pykes' operations on Kessel. He was killed in a raid on the mines that sparked a slave uprising and droid revolution. The damage to the mines and the loss of coaxium cut into the Pykes' profits and upset the galactic underworld's delicate balance of power.

TECHNOLOGY

COAXIUM

On Kessel, spice is king but coaxium is queen. Coaxium is a form of hypermatter that straddles the boundary between realspace and hyperspace, and an essential fuel for faster-than-light travel. It's mined on Kessel and then carefully transferred to refineries for processing. Unrefined coaxium is extremely volatile, and will explode if it gets too cold or is violently jostled. One of the Empire's early priorities was taking control of coaxium production to ensure sufficient fuel for its starfleet.

DROIDS

L3-37

A cantankerous droid who assembled herself, L3-37 traveled the galaxy with Lando Calrissian, who benefited from her extraordinary navigational database. A fiery advocate for droid rights, L3 was destroyed on Kessel while leading a droid revolt, but lived on as one of the droid brains operating the *Millennium Falcon*.

DD-BD

Adminmechs oversee other droids and perform clerical work, and often serve corporations in industrial settings. A WDD adminmech, DD-BD found himself bought at an auction by the Pykes and put to work on Kessel. Freed of his restraining bolt by L3-37, DD-BD eagerly joined her rebellion against the planet's cruel Pyke overseers.

WEAPON

A300 BLASTER RIFLE

BlasTech's A300 rifle is seen across the galaxy because it's cheap and easy to operate and maintain. That made it a good fit for Pyke operations on Kessel, where toxic air and ever-present dust were a constant headache, shortening the operational life of weapons and equipment.

TAK

There are many ways to wind up a prisoner on Kessel, doomed to work until killed by exhaustion, accident, or the rumored perils of the Dark. Tak made a dishonest living fleecing the elderly on Coruscant, but was caught trying to swindle the princess of Kessel and clapped into the mines.

SAGWA

Hailing from the Wookiee city of Rwookrrorro on Kashyyyk, Sagwa fought back against an Imperial patrol and found himself with a one-way ticket to Kessel's infamous spice mines. Fortunately for Sagwa, Chewbacca found him and freed him, and the two fought side by side against the Pykes' sentinels.

NEW TERRITORIES

YAVIN 4

An emerald moon orbiting a gas giant in a
lonely corner of the Outer Rim, Yavin 4 was
known only to scouts and gas prospectors
until the Alliance chose it as its principal base.
Rebel starfighters destroyed the Death Star at
Yavin 4, striking a blow for galactic freedom.

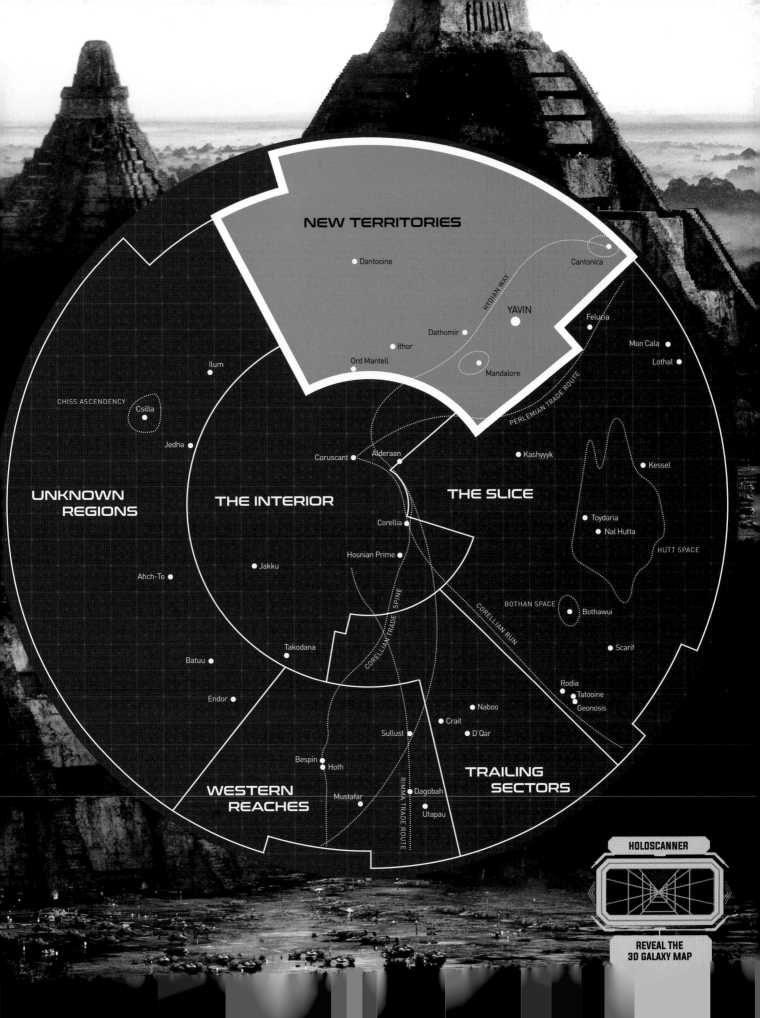

YAVIN 4

PLANETARY DATA

SECTOR: Gordian Reach

SYSTEM: Yavin

TYPE: Terrestrial

CLIMATE: Temperate

DIAMETER: 10,200 km

TERRAIN: Jungle, rainforest

ROTATION PERIOD: 24 standard hours

ORBITAL PERIOD: 4,818 local rotations

SENTIENT SPECIES: None

POPULATION: 1,000 (estimated)

SECTION THREE

YAVIN 4

WHERE HOPE WAS REBORN

YAVIN 4 IS A JUNGLE MOON ORBITING A GAS GIANT IN A BACKWATER CORNER OF THE OUTER RIM. YET THIS EMERALD WORLD WAS THE SITE OF AN EVENT THAT WOULD RESHAPE GALACTIC HISTORY. THE REBEL ALLIANCE CHOSE YAVIN 4 AS ITS PRINCIPAL HEADQUARTERS, AND LEIA ORGANA BROUGHT THE STOLEN DEATH STAR PLANS THERE FOR ANALYSIS SOON AFTER THE BATTLE OF SCARIF. THE IMPERIAL BATTLE STATION TRACKED HER, INTENDING TO DESTROY THE MOON AND THE REBELLION WITH A SINGLE SHOT, BUT WAS INSTEAD DESTROYED ITSELF BY LUKE SKYWALKER, WHO FIRED A PROTON TORPEDO FROM HIS X-WING FIGHTER. THIS UNLIKELY VICTORY SHOOK IMPERIAL RULE TO ITS VERY FOUNDATIONS.

OVERVIEW

THE GREAT TEMPLE • MASSASSI VALLEY • SKYGAZER HILL

HISTORY

An obscure Outer Rim moon, Yavin 4 was host to the Alliance's principal base, and was the site of the destruction of the first Death Star, a victory that brought a new hope to the galaxy.

ᴅᴠᴎᵞᴑᴄᴠᴉ ᴊᴑ ᴠᴋᵞᴉᴎ 4

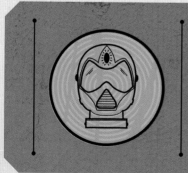

DK-RA-43'S COMMENT

"Perhaps you've just worn me down, but this destination has actual historical merit and its ecosystem isn't so hostile that we'll be devoured the moment we disembark. That said, we must be cautious if exploring the dangerous areas I know you'll want to visit. The rebels left munitions behind when they evacuated their base, and the Death Star debris field is both a navigational hazard and prowled by scavengers who shoot first and ask questions never."

THE GREAT TEMPLE

The ancient stone temples that dot Yavin 4's jungles are all that remain of the vanished Massassi culture. Rebel scouts surveyed Yavin 4 as a possible base, and the Alliance leadership fled there after being forced to abandon Dantooine. The Great Temple was built from giant blocks of stone, making it strong enough to resist orbital bombardment by Imperial capital ships – though not a strike from the Death Star's superlaser.

WEAPONS

E-11 BLASTER RIFLE

Standard issue for the Galactic Empire's stormtroopers, the BlasTech E-11 blaster rifle featured a telescopic sight and a high powered, red colored plasma bolt. Many were seized by members of the Rebellion and used against their former owners.

A WORLD BRIMMING WITH LIFE

Yavin 4 is home to a few hardy settlers and visited by scavengers and the occasional intrepid tourist with an interest in history. While services are all but nonexistent, nature-lovers have explored the moon's lush jungles and river valleys. Yavin 4 is a wild place where a traveler must take care, but it lacks large predators that might see incautious trekkers as an opportunity for an easy meal.

STARLOFT TRANSPORT

R 2

TO YAVIN IV

YAV

Position/Flight
8D8 IG/88

PERSONS OF INTEREST

LEIA ORGANA

The daughter of Anakin Skywalker and Padmé Amidala, Leia's origins were kept secret and she was raised by Bail and Breha Organa on Alderaan. There, she became an Imperial senator and a key leader of the Rebel Alliance. Her fight for freedom spanned decades, as she served the Alliance, the New Republic, and then the Resistance.

JYN ERSO

The daughter of an Imperial researcher, Jyn Erso served with Saw Gerrera's partisans before making her own way in a hostile galaxy. On Yavin 4, Erso pleaded with the rebels to take the fight to the Empire, with clandestine holos of her impassioned speech inspiring many new recruits.

POE DAMERON

Poe Dameron is one of the Resistance's best starfighter pilots, noted for leading the raid that destroyed the First Order's Starkiller Base and for his valor at Takodana, D'Qar, and Crait. Before becoming a New Republic pilot, Dameron grew up on Yavin 4, the son of two rebel veterans of the Battle of Endor.

DROIDS

K-2SO

A reprogrammed Imperial security droid, K-2SO made an ideal rebel agent, assisting Cassian Andor on many missions against the Empire. The sardonic Arakyd Industries droid was destroyed in the rebel raid on Scarif, but played a vital role in securing the plans for the Death Star battle station.

R2-BHD

The Alliance's starfighter pilots rely on astromechs while behind the sticks of X-wings and Y-wings, with droids performing repairs and optimizing systems. In such situations, pilots and astromechs often form lasting bonds. On Yavin 4, R2-BHD usually flew with Jon Vander, the leader of Gold Squadron's Y-wings.

HOLOSCANNER

VICTORY STATION (NOW CLOSED)

Scavengers began searching the wreckage of the Death Star soon after the Battle of Yavin, playing hide-and-seek with Imperial patrols tasked with safeguarding the debris. For a brief time after the New Republic's victory at Endor, entrepreneurs offered tours of the battlefield from a habitat they called Victory Station. The station closed long ago, and was quickly stripped for more salvage.

The workhorse starfighter of the Rebel Alliance and the New Republic, the X-wing is nimble enough to survive dogfights with TIE fighters and powerful enough to take on capital ships, making it a formidable asset in aerial combat. The X-wing's history dates back to the Z-95 and ARC-170 fighters of the Republic era.

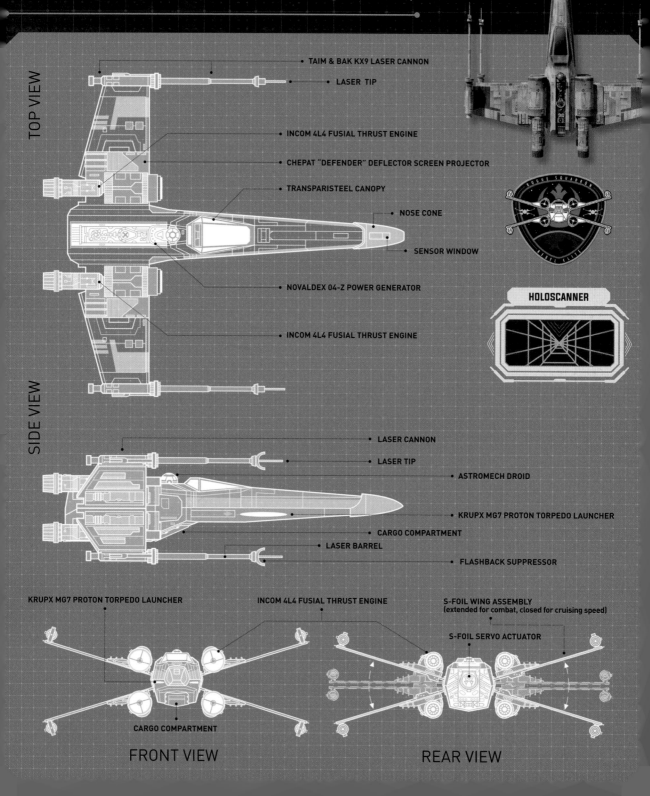

TOP VIEW

TAIM & BAK KX9 LASER CANNON

LASER TIP

INCOM 4L4 FUSIAL THRUST ENGINE

CHEPAT "DEFENDER" DEFLECTOR SCREEN PROJECTOR

TRANSPARISTEEL CANOPY

NOSE CONE

SENSOR WINDOW

NOVALDEX 04-Z POWER GENERATOR

INCOM 4L4 FUSIAL THRUST ENGINE

HOLOSCANNER

SIDE VIEW

LASER CANNON

LASER TIP

ASTROMECH DROID

KRUPX MG7 PROTON TORPEDO LAUNCHER

CARGO COMPARTMENT

LASER BARREL

FLASHBACK SUPPRESSOR

KRUPX MG7 PROTON TORPEDO LAUNCHER

INCOM 4L4 FUSIAL THRUST ENGINE

S-FOIL WING ASSEMBLY
(extended for combat, closed for cruising speed)

S-FOIL SERVO ACTUATOR

CARGO COMPARTMENT

FRONT VIEW

REAR VIEW

U-WING STARFIGHTER

Though classified as a starfighter, the U-wing served the Alliance and New Republic as a troop transport and gunship, delivering troops to battlefields under heavy fire. U-wings can absorb a lot of punishment, relying on their armor and deflector shields – which are strengthened with the craft's S-foils spread in their wide-swept defensive configuration.

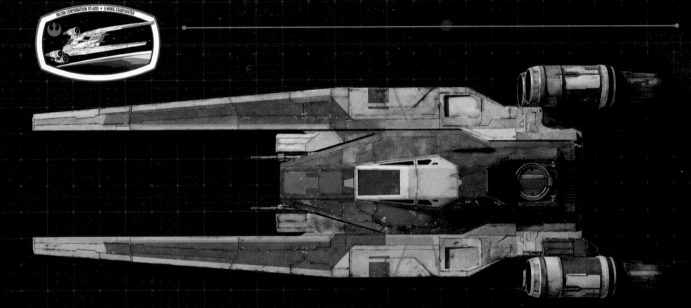

BLOCKADE RUNNER

Corellian corvettes are common sights in the galaxy, combining speed and defensive capabilities. The *Tantive IV* served both Bail Organa and his daughter Leia. It carried the rebel plans away from Scarif, only to be captured by Darth Vader above Tatooine.

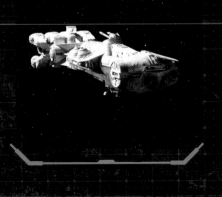

Y-WING STARFIGHTER

Designed for the Republic as a long-range bomber, the Y-wing found a new lease on life with the Alliance as a slow but sturdy starfighter. For easier maintenance, rebel mechanics stripped off the fairing enclosing their ion engines and components. Yavin 4's Gold Squadron consisted of twelve Y-wings, which fought at Scarif and above the Death Star.

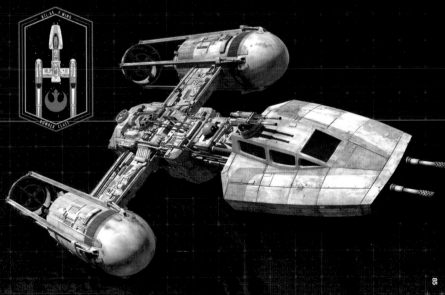

TRAILING SECTORS

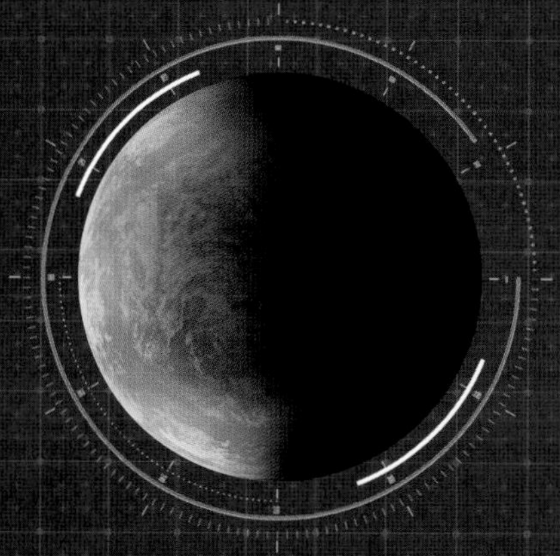

NABOO

A graceful, beautiful world in the Mid Rim, Naboo is home to both the native Gungans and human immigrants. It's known for its art and architecture, as well as the skill of its diplomats and negotiators.

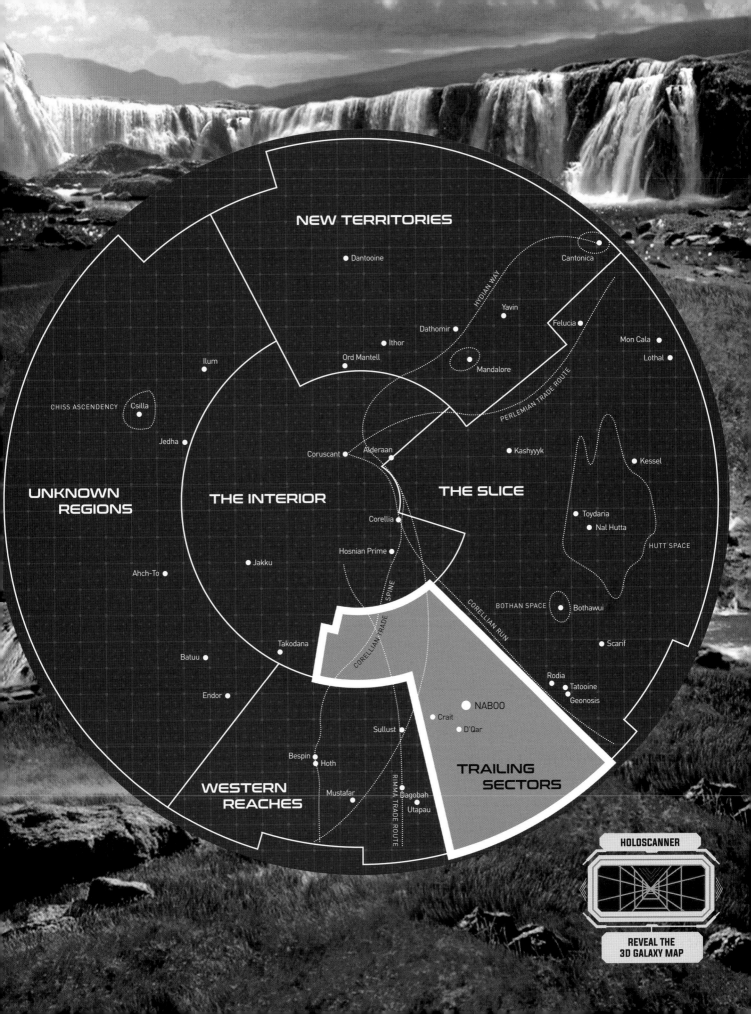

NEW TERRITORIES

- Dantooine
- Cantonica
- Yavin
- Dathomir
- Felucia
- Ithor
- Mon Cala
- Ord Mantell
- Lothal
- Mandalore
- Ilum

HYDIAN WAY

PERLEMIAN TRADE ROUTE

CHISS ASCENDENCY
- Csilla
- Jedha

- Coruscant
- Alderaan
- Kashyyyk
- Kessel

UNKNOWN REGIONS

THE INTERIOR

THE SLICE

- Corellia
- Toydaria
- Nal Hutta

- Hosnian Prime

HUTT SPACE

- Jakku
- Ahch-To

CORELLIAN TRADE SPINE

CORELLIAN RUN

BOTHAN SPACE
- Bothawui

- Takodana
- Scarif
- Batuu

- Rodia
- Tatooine
- Geonosis

- Endor

- NABOO
- Crait
- Sullust
- D'Qar

- Bespin
- Hoth

RIMMA TRADE ROUTE

WESTERN REACHES

TRAILING SECTORS

- Mustafar
- Dagobah
- Utapau

HOLOSCANNER

REVEAL THE 3D GALAXY MAP

312

NABOO

PLANETARY DATA

SECTOR: Chommell

TYPE: Terrestrial

CLIMATE: Temperate

DIAMETER: 12,120 km

TERRAIN: Mountains, plains, swamps

ROTATION PERIOD: 26 standard hours

ORBITAL PERIOD: 312 local rotations

SENTIENT SPECIES: Gungans

POPULATION: 4.5 billion

NABOO

A GRACEFUL, PEACEFUL WORLD WITH BEAUTIFUL CITIES BUILT BY BOTH HUMANS AND GUNGANS, NABOO HAS BEEN AN UNLIKELY FULCRUM IN GALACTIC HISTORY, AS IT IS THE HOMEWORLD TO BOTH SENATOR PADMÉ AMIDALA AND EMPEROR PALPATINE. QUICK ACTION BY THE NEW REPUBLIC AND ITS OWN ROYAL DEFENDERS ALLOWED IT TO ESCAPE PALPATINE'S WRATH AFTER THE BATTLE OF ENDOR. THE NABOO HAVE A LONG TRADITION OF USING DOUBLES AND DECOYS IN EVERYTHING FROM THEIR ART TO THEIR DIPLOMACY, AND VISITORS TO THIS LOVELY WORLD SHOULD ALWAYS BE PREPARED TO LOOK DEEPER IN SEARCH OF ELUSIVE TRUTHS.

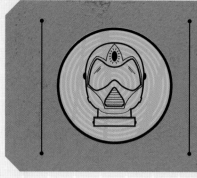

DK-RA-43'S COMMENT

"At long last, a civilized planet where one is unlikely to be devoured or kidnapped by slavers! Naboo is a world that cares deeply about the arts, and I could create a two-week itinerary solely around its museums, parklands, and architecture. The traditions of the Gungans are intriguing as well, fusing modern technology with biomechanics to create aesthetically pleasing underwater cities. So why do I suspect we'll spend our entire time dodging death in the planet core?"

OVERVIEW

GUNGAN HIGH COUNCIL • OTOH GUNGA • THEED • NABOO ABYSS • LAKE COUNTRY • VARYKINO • FESTIVAL OF LIGHT

HISTORY

Human colonists came to Naboo millennia ago from the Core Worlds, creating graceful cities and striking an uneasy truce with the planet's native Gungans. The Trade Federation's blockade of Naboo led to the ascension of its Senator Palpatine as chancellor and then Emperor.

SPECIES

GUNGANS

Gungans' flexible bones, prehensile tongues, and strong bills make them superbly adapted for amphibious life. They are homebodies, preferring their graceful underwater cities to life elsewhere on Naboo or visits to other planets. Gungan armies helped defend the planet against the Trade Federation's droids, leading to better relations with the Naboo settlers.

CREATURES

FAMBAA

Huge, powerful amphibians, fambaas are born with moist skins and gills, but as they mature the gills vanish and the skin dries and thickens. Gungans make use of fambaas as both beasts of burden and draft beasts for artillery, breeding herds in secret swamp pastures located deep within their sacred places.

TRANSPORT (STRAP) TAG

NABOO

TO

NAB

FROM COR. TENDER N1

VISIT THE GALAXY'S PASTORAL PARADISE VIA:

ROYAL NUBIAN LINES

T 14 J-327

SHAAK

These rotund herbivores are prized by the Naboo and Gungans for their meat, hides, and fatty ambergris. The ambergris makes shaaks quite buoyant – entire herds have survived accidental trips over Naboo waterfalls, disoriented and upset but otherwise unharmed.

THE LAKE COUNTRY

Naboo's Lake Country is a pastoral region of farms and meadowlands dotted with chains of lakes and soaring waterfalls. The planet's artists, royalty, and old families leave the (relative) hustle-bustle of Theed and Moenia for tranquil weekends at lakeside estates such as Varykino, the long-time island retreat of the famous Naberrie family. An ideal time to visit the Lake Country is during the springtime Festival of Glad Arrival, when musicians, artists, and acting troupes stage pageants and performances.

CREATURES

SANDO AQUA MONSTER

While Naboo's forests and plains are largely peaceful, its honeycomb planet core is a dangerous region, a bewildering labyrinth prowled by vicious creatures. The unquestioned alpha predator of the so-called Naboo Abyss is the sando aqua monster, a massive mammal that can reach more than 200 meters in length. Sando aqua monsters prey on colo claw fish and opee sea killers, both formidable predators in their own right.

OPEE SEA KILLER

A curious creature with aspects of both crustaceans and fish, the opee sea killer dwells in the Naboo Abyss, where it attracts prey with phosphorescent lures on the tips of its antennae and captures them with a long, sticky tongue that can extend three times its body length, sweeping up schools of fish in a gulp.

PADMÉ AMIDALA

Queen Amidala led the resistance to the Trade Federation's invasion of Naboo, then succeeded Palpatine as its senator when he became chancellor, with the two becoming political opponents. She died under mysterious circumstances soon after the birth of the Empire and was laid to rest on Naboo.

ROGUES' GALLERY

SHEEV PALPATINE

An undistinguished senator from a Mid Rim world, Sheev Palpatine rose to become Chancellor of the Republic during the Naboo Crisis, then led the galaxy through the horrors of the Clone Wars. After surviving an attempt on his life by the Jedi, he declared himself ruler of the First Galactic Empire.

DARTH MAUL

Apprentice to Darth Sidious, Darth Maul killed Qui-Gon Jinn on Naboo and was in turn slain by Obi-Wan Kenobi – or so the Jedi believed. In reality, Maul's rage, will, and Force powers allowed the renegade Sith to survive. He seized control of Mandalore during the Clone Wars and became the leader of the shadowy crime syndicate known as Crimson Dawn.

VEHICLES

NABOO STARFIGHTER

N-1 STARFIGHTER

The Naboo believe machines should be beautiful as well as functional, and their sleek, deadly starfighters embody this belief, tucking advanced starfighter capabilities inside a graceful, custom-built spaceframe. The N-1's chromium finish indicates royal status; on Naboo, colors and materials always convey meaning about objects' purpose and history.

NABOO ROYAL STARSHIP

Handcrafted by Naboo shipbuilders, the gleaming royal starship was built to carry the planet's rulers around Naboo and on state visits and trips to Coruscant. Queen Amidala fled the Trade Federation blockade of her planet aboard her royal starship, arriving at Coruscant after a leaking hyperdrive forced her to divert to Tatooine to make repairs.

NABOO ROYAL CRUISER

After Padmé Amidala left office as queen and became Naboo's senator, Queen Réillata allowed her to use a starship with the chrome plating traditionally reserved for monarchs. The Naboo cruiser was better defended than previous royal starships, with potent deflector shields, a backup hyperdrive, and recharge sockets for a quartet of N-1 starfighters.

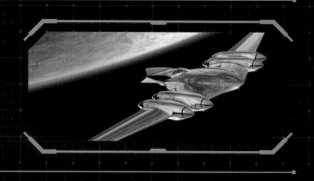

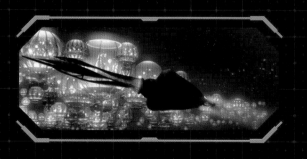

BONGO

Like many Gungan designs, the bongo is shaped by nature as well as technology, combining an organically grown shell with mechanical components. These submersibles are common sights in the Gungans' underwater cities, carrying passengers as well as cargo. Rotating fins drive the craft through the water, with buoyancy maintained via spongelike hydrostatic chambers.

WEAPONS

ELG-3A BLASTER

Elegant yet deadly, the ELG-3A was used by Padmé Amidala and her handmaidens when they retook Theed's royal palace from the Trade Federation's battle droids. Two ELG-3As were kept hidden in the queen's throne for use in emergencies.

DROIDS

DESTROYER DROID

B-1s were disposable shock troops, but the Colicoid-designed destroyer droids proved deadly on Naboo and during the Clone Wars. "Droidekas" rolled into battle in wheel mode, then unfurled their powerful blaster cannons and activated shield envelopes. Even Jedi Masters respected their destructive potential.

HOLOSCANNER

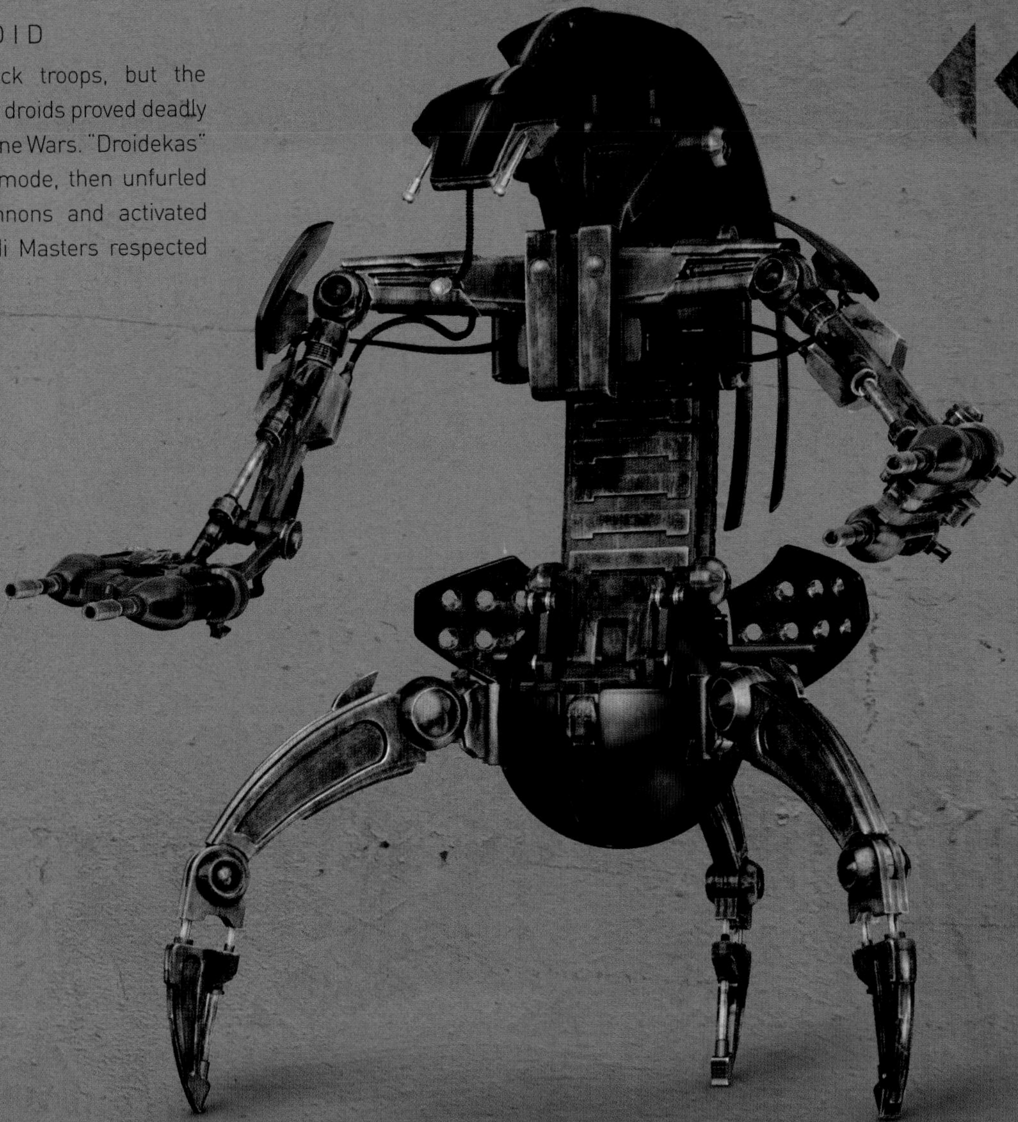

DARTH MAUL'S LIGHTSABER

The Sith warrior Darth Maul fought with a rare double-bladed lightsaber – an ungainly weapon that compelled him to push his physical and Force abilities to their highest potential.

SITH

WESTERN REACHES

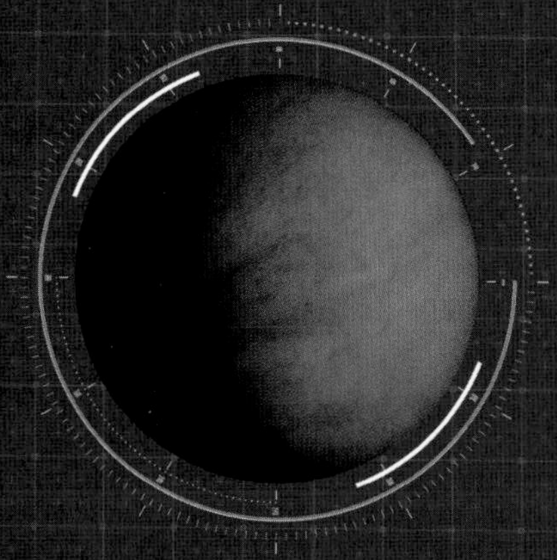

BESPIN

A gas giant in the Outer Rim, Bespin is home to the floating metropolis Cloud City, a resort aerie that hid a profitable tibanna gas mine. This planet was the site of a fateful confrontation between Luke Skywalker and Darth Vader not long after the Battle of Hoth.

HOTH

An obscure ice ball, Hoth was chosen as the site of a key rebel base after the Battle of Yavin. Rebel forces struggled to adapt their equipment to the planet's brutal climate, and then were discovered and routed in battle by Imperial forces led by Darth Vader.

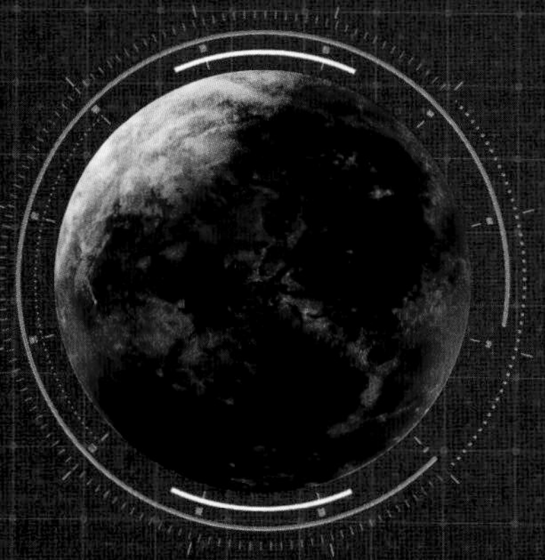

MUSTAFAR

A hellish volcanic world, Mustafar houses mining facilities and became infamous as the personal retreat of Darth Vader. Jedi fugitives knew it as the place where they went to die, broken in interrogation by the Emperor's feared cadre of dark side Inquisitors.

NEW TERRITORIES

- Dantooine
- Cantonica
- Yavin
- Dathomir
- Felucia
- Mon Cala
- Ithor
- Lothal
- Ord Mantell
- Mandalore
- Ilum
- CHISS ASCENDENCY · Csilla
- Kashyyyk
- Kessel
- Jedha
- Coruscant · Alderaan

UNKNOWN
REGIONS

THE INTERIOR

THE SLICE

- Corellia
- Toydaria
- Nal Hutta
- Hosnian Prime
- HUTT SPACE
- Jakku
- Ahch-To
- BOTHAN SPACE · Bothawui
- Scarif
- Takodana
- Batuu
- Rodia
- Tatooine
- Endor
- Geonosis
- Naboo
- Crait
- Sullust
- D'Qar
- BESPIN
- HOTH
- TRAILING
SECTORS
- MUSTAFAR
- WESTERN
REACHES
- Dagobah
- Utapau

HYDIAN WAY

PERLEMIAN TRADE ROUTE

CORELLIAN TRADE SPINE

CORELLIAN RUN

RIMMA TRADE ROUTE

HOLOSCANNER

REVEAL THE
3D GALAXY MAP

BESPIN

PLANETARY DATA

SECTOR: Anoat

TYPE: Gas Giant

CLIMATE: Temperate (in Life Zone)

DIAMETER: 118,000 km

TERRAIN: N/A

ROTATION PERIOD: 12 standard hours

ORBITAL PERIOD: 5,110 local rotations

SENTIENT SPECIES: None

POPULATION: 6 million

SECTION FIVE

BESPIN

FOR DECADES, THE FLOATING METROPOLIS CLOUD CITY HID AN INTRIGUING SECRET. THE FACILITY WAS KNOWN AS A LUXURY RESORT ATTRACTING HIGH-ROLLERS AND RICH TOURISTS TO THE GAS GIANT BESPIN, BUT ITS REAL WEALTH CAME FROM MINING TIBANNA GAS, A LUCRATIVE ENTERPRISE CONDUCTED QUIETLY TO ESCAPE NOTICE BY THE MINING GUILD AND THE EMPIRE. THE ARRANGEMENT WAS HONED TO PERFECTION UNDER THE PROFITABLE ADMINISTRATION OF LANDO CALRISSIAN, BUT THE GOOD TIMES ENDED WHEN DARTH VADER PURSUED REBEL FUGITIVES TO BESPIN. VADER LEFT A GARRISON BEHIND, AND CLOUD CITY SUFFERED UNDER A FANATICAL IMPERIAL GOVERNOR UNTIL ITS LIBERATION USHERED IN A NEWLY PROFITABLE ERA.

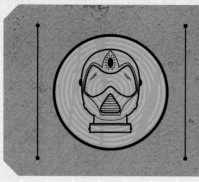

DK-RA-43'S COMMENT

"Sunsets on Bespin are glorious, and Cloud City offers a wealth of creature comforts for civilized travelers. I don't know what the fuss is about all this mining business, though. It sounds terribly dull, not to mention dirty. And for all its beauty, Cloud City has no real history. It's only a few centuries old, and most of its existence has been spent making credits. How crass! Still, the views will be exciting even when the conversation's dull."

ᗡᐯᑎᒍᕼᐁᒐᐯᎸ ᒍᗡ ᘓᐯᑎᐯᑌᎸᐯ

OVERVIEW

CLOUD CITY • UGNAUGHT SURFACE • UGNORGRAD
• PORT TOWN • TIBBANNOPOLIS

HISTORY

Founded by a Corellian hyperspace scout turned entrepreneur, Cloud City is simultaneously a resort and a lucrative tibanna gas mine – which makes it an excellent place to strike a deal, hit it big, or both.

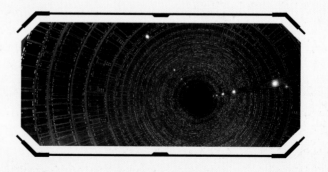

Cloud City hovers in Bespin's Life Zone, a thin slice where the atmosphere is breathable and conditions are temperate. The upper levels are dotted with casinos, hotels and luxe eateries, while the lower levels are dedicated to the processing of tibanna gas. These levels are decidedly unglamorous, filled with machinery and dormitories for Cloud City's Ugnaught workforce. A few adventurous tourists tour the processing works or explore Cloud City's seedy Port Town district.

SPECIES

UGNAUGHTS

A porcine species from Gentes, Ugnaughts do much of the work on Cloud City, and have earned a reputation as hard workers who do dirty and tough jobs without complaint. Bespin's Ugnaughts have lived on Cloud City since it was built. Clan leaders struck a deal with founder Ecclessis Figg to work in return for homes in his city and a share of the tibanna mining profits. Other Ugnaughts dwell in the Ugnaught Surface, a floating colony of their own.

ROGUES' GALLERY
BOBA FETT

A legendary bounty hunter, Boba Fett began his long career during the Clone Wars, as a child learning his trade from his father Jango and legendary rogues such as Aurra Sing, Cad Bane and Hondo Ohnaka. As a young man Fett led gangs of hunters, but he now prefers to work alone, holding to no code except how many credits a target is worth and the conditions for bringing in the bounty.

HOLOSCANNER

WEAPON

HAN SOLO'S BLASTER

A heavily modified version of the BlasTech DL-44 heavy blaster pistol, Han Solo used this as his sidearm of choice for more than 30 years, after it was given to him by veteran smuggler Tobias Beckett.

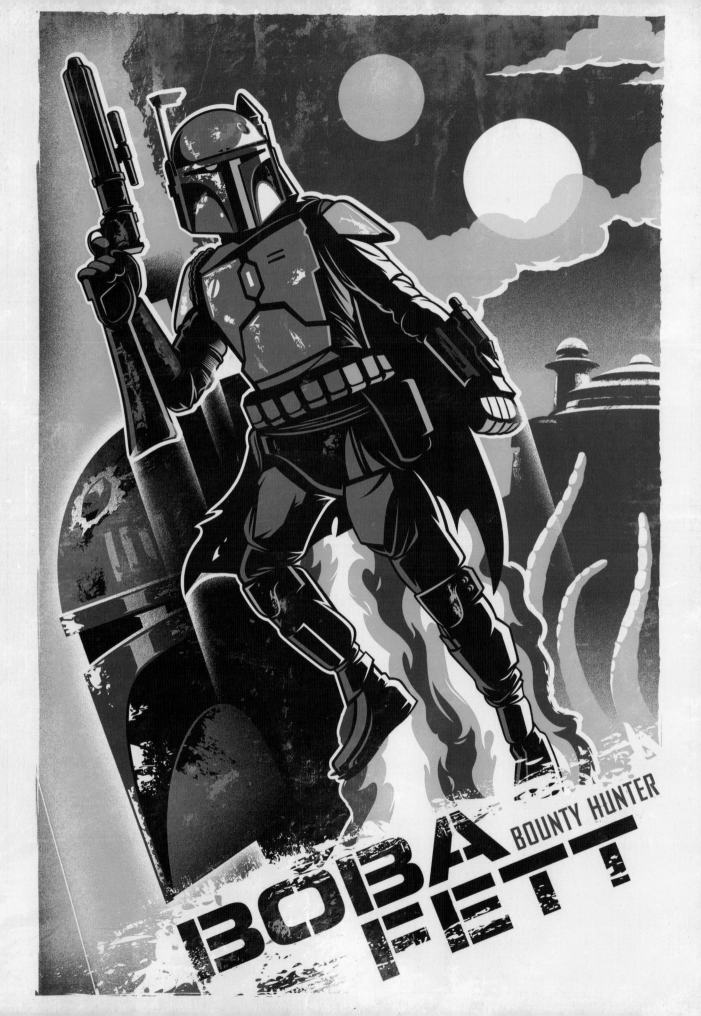

SLAVE I

A heavily modified *Firespray-31*-class patrol craft, *Slave I* served Jango Fett for years before becoming the property of Aurra Sing, Hondo Ohnaka, and then Boba Fett. Jango outfitted *Slave I* with blaster cannons, concussion missiles, and seismic charges; Boba then added special modifications of his own. A powerful sensor jammer allowed *Slave I* to go undetected by most scanners, letting Boba Fett approach his bounties without being detected.

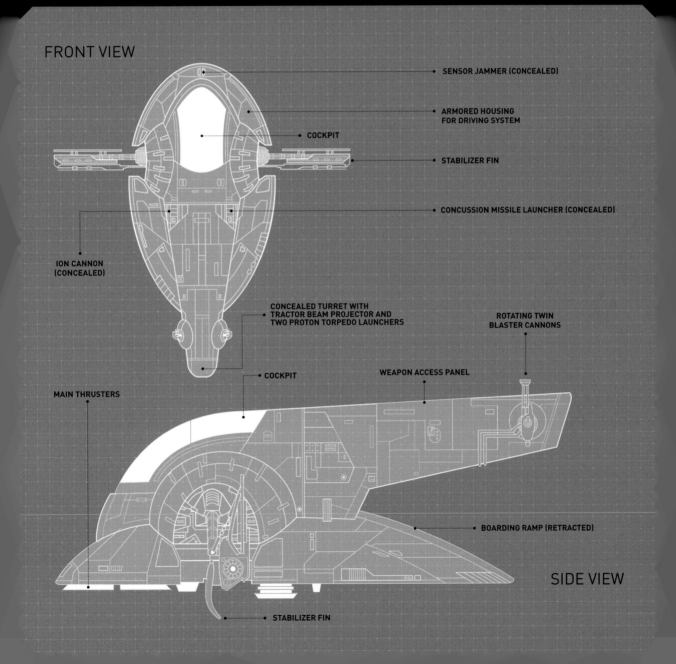

FRONT VIEW

SENSOR JAMMER (CONCEALED)

ARMORED HOUSING FOR DRIVING SYSTEM

COCKPIT

STABILIZER FIN

CONCUSSION MISSILE LAUNCHER (CONCEALED)

ION CANNON (CONCEALED)

CONCEALED TURRET WITH TRACTOR BEAM PROJECTOR AND TWO PROTON TORPEDO LAUNCHERS

ROTATING TWIN BLASTER CANNONS

MAIN THRUSTERS

COCKPIT

WEAPON ACCESS PANEL

BOARDING RAMP (RETRACTED)

SIDE VIEW

STABILIZER FIN

THE TWIN-POD CLOUD CAR

Wing Guard uses these small atmospheric craft to patrol above Cloud City. Each cloud car features a pilot and a gunner, who sit in separate pods, connected by a repulsorlift engine. Cloud cars only have light blaster cannons, so Wing Guard patrols are prepared to call for backup if outgunned by intruders.

CLOUD CITY SKYWAYS

WEIGHT THIS PIECE 3.27

FLIGHT ORIG. YAV.

TO: **BES**

BESPIN

PERSONS OF INTEREST

LANDO CALRISSIAN

Sportsman, smuggler, and self-professed scoundrel, Lando Calrissian was born on Socorro and enjoyed a happily misspent youth before losing his beloved starship, the *Millennium Falcon*, to Han Solo. Lando eventually went semi-respectable as Cloud City's administrator and returned to Bespin to help liberate it from Imperial captivity.

LOBOT

Lando's aide and friend, Lobot communicated with Cloud City's central computer through a AJ^6 cyborg construct. When Lando turned against the Empire, Lobot led the Wing Guard against the stormtroopers. He later played a key role in breaking the so-called Iron Blockade of the Anoat sector enforced by Governor Adelhard.

bespin

endless clouds in an astrophysical rarity

HOTH

PLANETARY DATA

SECTOR: Anoat

TYPE: Terrestrial

CLIMATE: Frigid

DIAMETER: 7,200 km

TERRAIN: Ice plains, mountains

ROTATION PERIOD: 23 standard hours

ORBITAL PERIOD: 549 local rotations

SENTIENT SPECIES: None

POPULATION: No permanent residents

SECTION FIVE

HOTH

AN ICE BALL TUCKED AWAY ON AN OFFSHOOT OF AN OUTER RIM HYPERSPACE LANE, HOTH SERVED THE REBEL ALLIANCE AS A NEW BASE AFTER THE BATTLE OF YAVIN BUT WAS SOON DISCOVERED BY THE EMPIRE. THE BATTLE OF HOTH WAS A MAJOR IMPERIAL VICTORY, THOUGH REBEL LEADERS SLIPPED THROUGH DARTH VADER'S DRAGNET. THE PLANET'S HOSTILE CONDITIONS PREVENTED SETTLEMENTS FROM TAKING ROOT BEFORE OR AFTER THE ALLIANCE'S TIME THERE, AND HOTH SOON RETURNED TO BEING ALL BUT IGNORED, REMEMBERED AS A FOOTNOTE IN GALACTIC HISTORY WHEN IT WAS RECALLED AT ALL.

OVERVIEW

ECHO BASE SITE • NEV ICE FLOE BATTLEFIELD
CLABBURN RANGE

HISTORY

The Rebel Alliance chose Hoth as the site of its new principal base after the Battle of Yavin but struggled to adapt to the icy world's punishing conditions. The Empire discovered the base and nearly destroyed the Alliance, whose top leaders barely escaped a ground assault by AT-ATs.

DK-RA-43'S COMMENT

"I must object! Hoth is an ice cube, intensely hostile to life (and proper droid function) and with little to interest even a masochistic explorer. Its battlefield was picked over decades ago; little remains to be seen except humps of snow and little remains to be found, except possibly unexploded ordnance (which no sane being wants to discover!) If you want to visit a war museum, I suggest the Uquine Memorial Orbital Site or the Mittoblade Hall of Remembrance. Both are excellent, and you won't freeze to death."

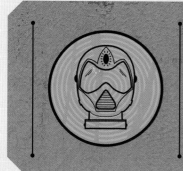

CREATURES

TAUNTAUN

These grumpy, odoriferous reptomammals live in herds, surviving on lichen and algae dug from beneath the snowpack. After dark, tauntauns seek shelter in glacier caves or dig out insulating snow caves. Their superb sense of smell allows them to detect hunting wampas and find underground grottos warmed by geothermal energy. These subterranean garden spots serve as lush refuges for breeding and raising young.

WAMPA

Hoth's apex predator, the wampa is a stealthy hunter that seeks out tauntauns, ice scrabblers, and other fauna of Hoth. Wampas use their powerful clawed paws to kill prey or batter victims unconscious to be eaten later. They use their cave dens as macabre larders, impaling prey on icicles and stalactites or sticking them fast in ceiling ice.

HOLOSCANNER

ROGUES' GALLERY

MAXIMILIAN VEERS

An Imperial veteran from Denon, General Veers fought for the Empire in campaigns such as Zaloriis and Culroon before being assigned to Darth Vader's Death Squadron. He led the AT-AT assault on Hoth's Echo Base, a major victory that nearly obliterated a key cell of the Rebel Alliance.

PERSON OF INTEREST

GENERAL RIEEKAN

A native of Alderaan, Carlist Rieekan was offworld when the Death Star destroyed his home planet, but the experience deeply marked him, turning him into a stern commander who vowed never to let those under his protection be left helpless again. Rieekan commanded Alliance forces at Echo Base and continued the fight as an officer in the New Republic.

ALL-TERRAIN ARMORED TRANSPORT

The Empire valued AT-ATs as both ground assault vehicles and instruments of terror; with the ground shaking around them and massive war machines looming above them, many Imperial adversaries simply surrendered. On Hoth, AT-ATs led the assault on Echo Base, complemented by two-legged AT-STs and snowtroopers on cold-adapted speeder bikes.

AT-AT

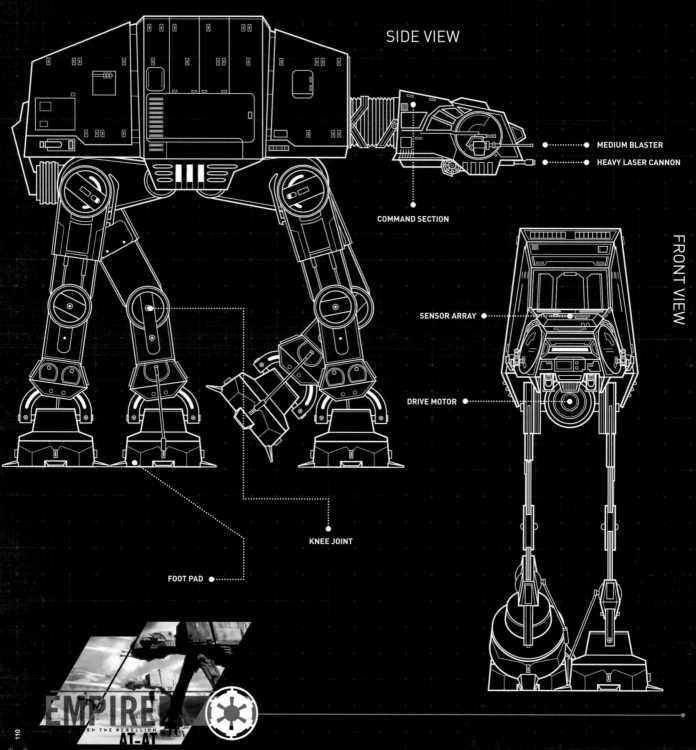

SIDE VIEW

MEDIUM BLASTER

HEAVY LASER CANNON

COMMAND SECTION

FRONT VIEW

SENSOR ARRAY

DRIVE MOTOR

KNEE JOINT

FOOT PAD

EMPIRE

AT-AT

DROIDS

IMPERIAL PROBE DROID

Arakyd's probes were engineered for both patrol and reconnaissance missions. The 11-3K model was well-suited for investigation and guarding Imperial facilities, while the Viper probe (depicted) deployed from hyperspace pods, searching for signs of habitation.

2-1B SURGICAL DROID

2-1B surgical droids have been common sights in the galaxy for generations, and are programmed to diagnose and treat injuries and illnesses that affect countless species. One 2-1B model supervised Luke Skywalker's recovery on Echo Base after Luke ran afoul of a wampa during a patrol on Hoth.

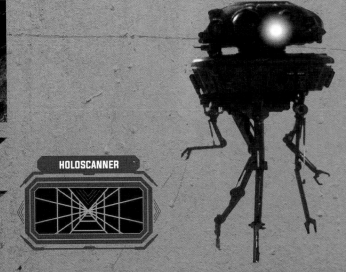

HOLOSCANNER

WEAPONS

A280 BLASTER RIFLE

A reliable rifle, BlasTech's A280 was a common sight in the rebel ranks on both Hoth and Endor.

V-150 PLANET DEFENDER

A powerful ion cannon with a spherical housing, the v-150 defended Hoth's Echo Base against Imperial attacks.

VEHICLES

GR-75 MEDIUM TRANSPORT

Slow and lightly armed, GR-75s were mainstays of the Alliance, ferrying personnel and goods between bases. Including being key to Echo Base's evacuation, they saw combat at Scarif and Endor.

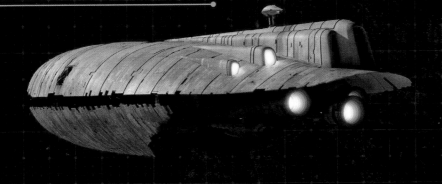

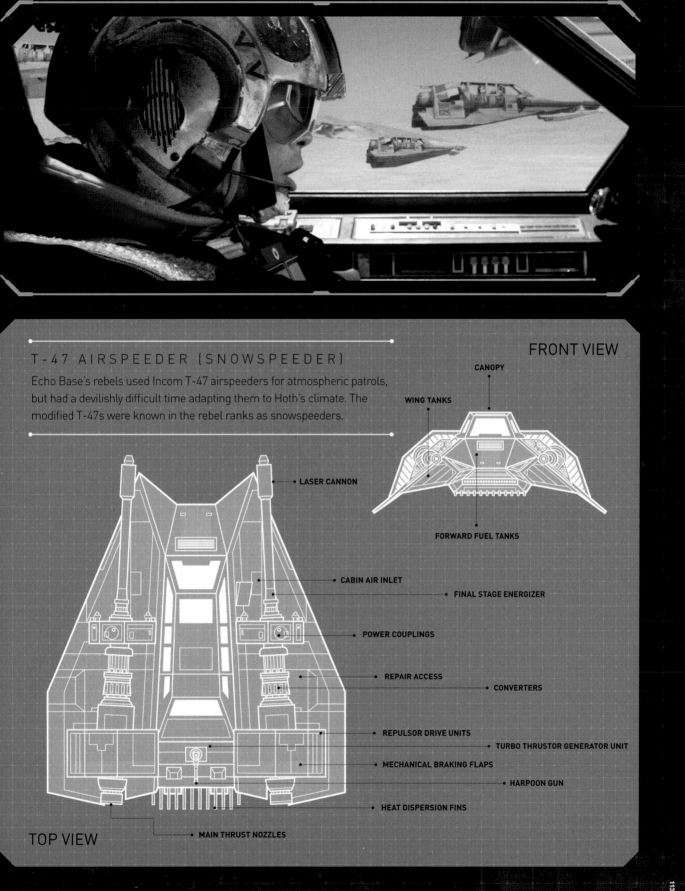

T-47 AIRSPEEDER (SNOWSPEEDER)

Echo Base's rebels used Incom T-47 airspeeders for atmospheric patrols, but had a devilishly difficult time adapting them to Hoth's climate. The modified T-47s were known in the rebel ranks as snowspeeders.

FRONT VIEW

CANOPY

WING TANKS

FORWARD FUEL TANKS

LASER CANNON

CABIN AIR INLET

FINAL STAGE ENERGIZER

POWER COUPLINGS

REPAIR ACCESS

CONVERTERS

REPULSOR DRIVE UNITS

TURBO THRUSTOR GENERATOR UNIT

MECHANICAL BRAKING FLAPS

HARPOON GUN

HEAT DISPERSION FINS

MAIN THRUST NOZZLES

TOP VIEW

412

MUSTAFAR

PLANETARY DATA

SECTOR: Atravis

TYPE: Terrestrial

CLIMATE: Hot

DIAMETER: 4,200 km

TERRAIN: Mountains, volcanoes

ROTATION PERIOD: 36 standard hours

ORBITAL PERIOD: 412 local rotations

SENTIENT SPECIES: Mustafarians

POPULATION: 20,000

MUSTAFAR

A HELLISH WORLD COVERED WITH SEAS OF BURNING LAVA, MUSTAFAR'S CRUST IS CONTINUALLY RESHAPED BY THE GRAVITY OF THE GAS GIANT JESTEFAD, WHOSE STRONG MAGNETIC FIELD ALSO SCOURS THE PLANET WITH FEROCIOUS ELECTRICAL STORMS. MINING FIRMS HAVE BRAVED THESE BRUTAL CONDITIONS FOR CENTURIES, BUILDING SHIELDED REFINERIES ON THE BLEAK OBSIDIAN SHORES OF MUSTAFAR'S BLAZING SEAS. IN A TESTAMENT TO THE TENACITY OF LIFE, MUSTAFAR HAS A NUMBER OF NATIVE SPECIES, INCLUDING THE INSECTOID BIPEDS KNOWN AS MUSTAFARIANS. MUSTAFARIANS LIVE IN CLANS, SEEKING HARMONY WITH THE SAVAGE NATURAL FORCES THAT HAVE SCULPTED THEIR BRUTAL HOMEWORLD.

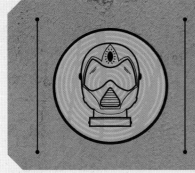

DK-RA-43'S COMMENT

"Maybe it's just that I'm programmed for logic while organic beings rather obviously aren't, but I tend to avoid places where my body is actually in danger of melting. And may I point out that members of your species suffer what you call "sunburns" from merely being outside in conditions where you actually evolved? Honestly, why don't we all jump in an industrial smelter? It would save time, and at least I'd die knowing my alloys would be recycled."

OVERVIEW

FRALIDEJA • ZITONTOWN • FORTRESS VADER • TULRUS ISLAND • GAHENN PLAINS • MENSIX MINING FACILITY

HISTORY

Once owned by the Techno Union, Mustafar was a hideout for the Separatists' leaders until they were apprehended at the end of the Clone Wars. The Empire restricted travel to the system.

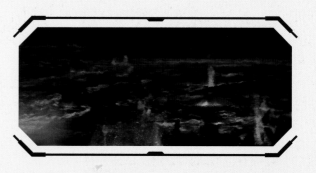

FORTRESS VADER

After the Separatists' defeat, the Empire awarded the Techno Union's refineries to the Mining Guild. But the Guild struggled to make Mustafar profitable, hampered by strict Imperial travel restrictions. Rumor had it that fugitive Jedi were sent to Mustafar for interrogation, never to return. No civilian traffic was allowed near Fortress Vader, an obsidian spike rising from the Gahenn Plains and used by Darth Vader as a private retreat.

DROIDS

INTERROGATION DROID

Developed in secret by the Imperial Department of Military Research, interrogator droids are used by the Empire to meticulously exploit a prisoner's mental and physical weaknesses. The floating, black mechanical menaces inject drugs that lessen pain tolerance and block mental resistance, and use hallucinogens and truth serums to influence victims. Only a select few have proven able to resist its excruciating methods.

HOLOSCANNER

DEPLOY THE
INTERROGATION DROID

mustafar

a tiny, fiery planet on the outer rim

HOLOSCANNER

LAVA FLEAS

These six-legged insects chew through Mustafar's crust, forming the cave complexes where Mustafarians live. Mustafarians use them as mounts and forge heat-resistant armor from their exoskeletons. Lava fleas are nimble and can leap 30 meters to escape gouts of upwelling lava.

MUSTAFARIANS

Mustafarians include two related subspecies: the lanky Northern Mustafarians and the stout, strong Southern Mustafarians. Both evolved from insect ancestors, and have hard shells that protect their leathery skins. The clans resent the presence of offworlders, but reluctantly struck a trade deal with the Techno Union centuries ago. Many Mustafarians served it and the Mining Guild as ore scouts, miners, and refinery laborers.

ROGUES' GALLERY

ANAKIN SKYWALKER/DARTH VADER

A terrifying figure in black armor, Darth Vader served the Empire as Palpatine's emissary and enforcer. Few knew he had once been Anakin Skywalker, hero of the Jedi Order and father of Luke Skywalker and Leia Organa. He died at Endor, having returned to the light and brought balance to the Force.

DARTH VADER'S LIGHTSABER

Jedi construct lightsabers by attuning themselves to kyber crystals, but the Sith technique is to corrupt an existing crystal and "bleed" it red. Darth Vader's saber had the crimson blade that was a Sith trademark.

MUSTAFARIAN MINING COMPLEX

At the end of the Clone Wars, the Separatist leaders sought refuge in an ore collection complex owned by the Techno Union. Republic agents discovered this hiding place and killed them, ending the galaxy-spanning conflict. The complex was then destroyed under circumstances that remain unclear. All intel about these incidents remains classified by the Empire, and is yet to be made public.

VEHICLE

DELTA-CLASS T-3C SHUTTLE

These bat-winged shuttles were never as popular as the more versatile
Lambda class, but Imperials such as Orson Krennic appreciated its stark,
brutal design. The Delta folds its wings to reduce space requirements in
hangars and on landing pads, and deploys them for greater stability during
atmospheric flight.

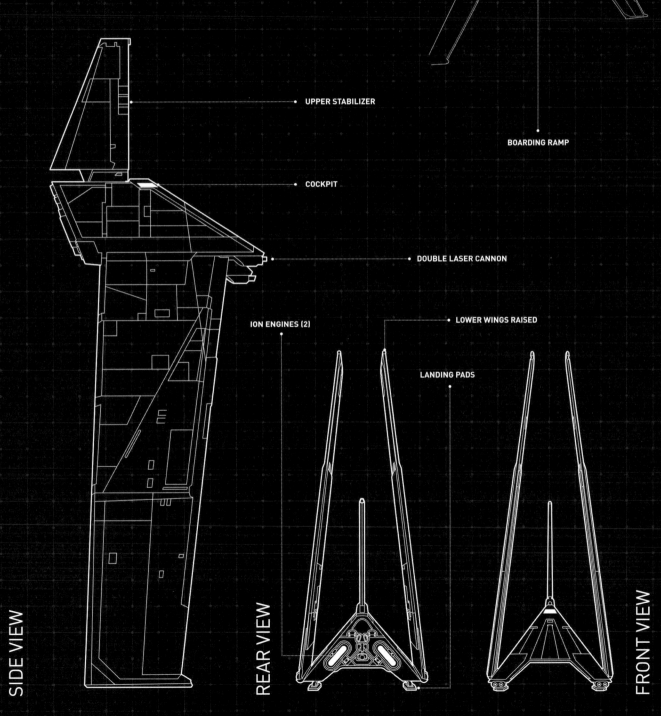

BOARDING RAMP

UPPER STABILIZER

COCKPIT

DOUBLE LASER CANNON

ION ENGINES (2)

LOWER WINGS RAISED

LANDING PADS

SIDE VIEW

REAR VIEW

FRONT VIEW

UNKNOWN REGIONS

ENDOR

The Emperor chose the Forest Moon of Endor as the construction site for the second Death Star, and lured the Alliance into a confrontation there. But thanks to the green moon's native Ewoks, the battle ended with Palpatine dead, the station destroyed, and Imperial rule in tatters.

STARKILLER BASE

The First Order secretly created Starkiller Base by coring a planet in the Unknown Regions and turning it into a superweapon able to destroy a star system halfway across the galaxy. Resistance starfighters destroyed Starkiller Base, but still had to face the First Order's massive war machine.

BATUU

Batuu sits on the edge of settled space, and for centuries was known only to intrepid scouts, traders, and those looking to disappear. In recent years it has become a center of intrigue, with agents of the First Order and the Resistance battling for position.

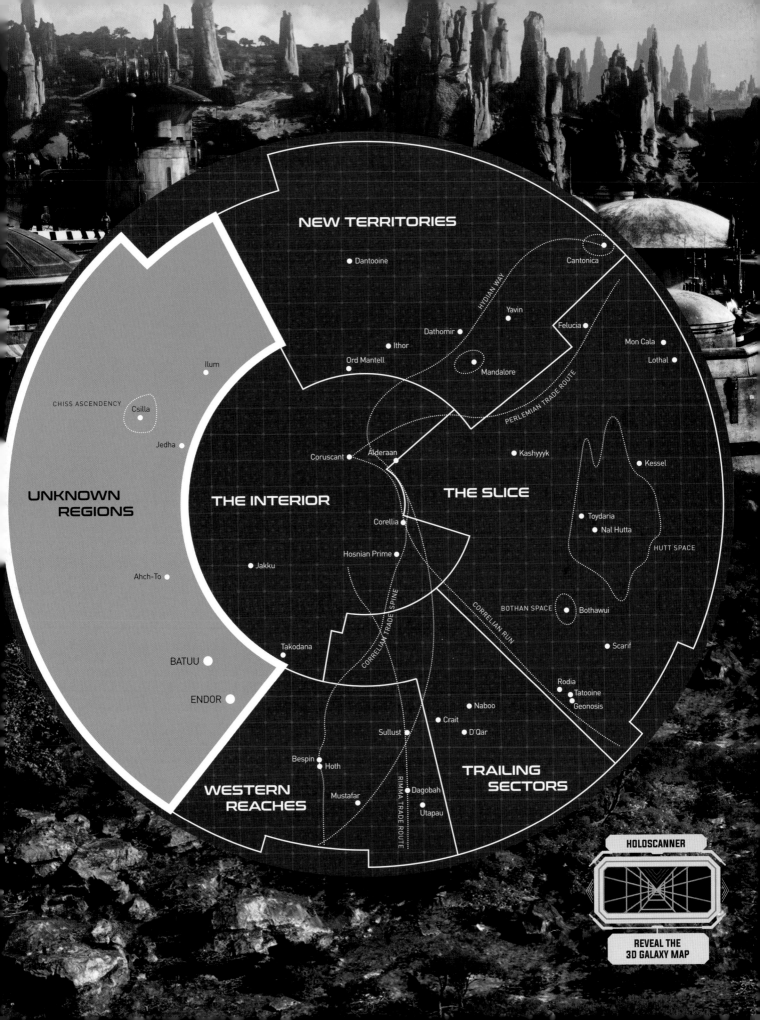

402

ENDOR

PLANETARY DATA

SECTOR: Moddell

TYPE: Terrestrial

CLIMATE: Temperate

DIAMETER: 4,900 km

TERRAIN: Forests, Savannas, Mountains

ROTATION PERIOD: 18 standard hours

ORBITAL PERIOD: 402 Local Rotations

SENTIENT SPECIES: Ewoks, Duloks, Yuzzum

POPULATION: 30 million

ENDOR

A PRISTINE GREEN GLOBE, THE FOREST MOON OF ENDOR LIES FAR FROM THE GALAXY'S BUSY PRECINCTS AND IS HOME TO THE EWOKS, METER-HIGH FURRED WARRIORS WHO DWELL IN TREETOP HUTS. THE EMPIRE CHOSE ENDOR AS THE CONSTRUCTION SITE FOR THE SECOND DEATH STAR AND LURED THE REBEL ALLIANCE THERE, LEADING TO THE CLIMACTIC BATTLE OF ENDOR. THE TIDE TURNED WHEN THE NATIVE EWOKS JOINED THE FIGHT, HELPING REBEL COMMANDOS BRING DOWN THE DEATH STAR'S DEFENCES. DESPITE BEING THE SITE OF FATEFUL EVENTS, ENDOR REMAINS REMOTE AND IS RARELY VISITED – A RELIEF FOR THE EWOKS WHO CALL IT HOME.

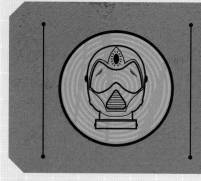

DK-RA-43'S COMMENT

"Oh good, another trip to the edge of the galaxy to look at wreckage. There's no spaceport, the local species lives in treehouses, and the forests are full of dangerous wildlife, but I'm sure it will be worthwhile to gaze upon a twisted, burned-out solar panel from a vintage TIE fighter. No, I will not be quiet! Have me sent for a memory wipe if you want, but this is absurd. If I were paranoid, I'd suspect this very strange galactic tour is actually cover for some nefarious business."

Welcome To
ENDOR
Visit our Lush Forest Moon.

OVERVIEW

ENDOR BUNKER • SHIELD GENERATOR • BRIGHT TREE VILLAGE

HISTORY

The Forest Moon of Endor circles a gas giant in a system near the galactic frontier. The Empire built the second Death Star in orbit above the moon, and the Alliance won its most important victory there, destroying the battle station and killing Emperor Palpatine.

EWOKS

These furry, meter-high bipeds may look like cuddly toys, but they're fierce warriors, defending their tribal territories with bows, spears and clever traps. Most dwell in villages of treetop huts, living in harmony with nature. While not technologically sophisticated, Ewoks are cunning warriors – as the Empire discovered to its regret. Since the Alliance's victory at Endor, a few curious Ewoks have left their homeworld to explore the galaxy.

ENDOR
HOME OF THE EWOKS

YUZZUM

The Ewoks aren't the only sentient species to dwell on the Forest Moon. The Yuzzum are furry, peaceable plains dwellers with rotund bodies atop long spindly legs. A few adventurous Yuzzum have left Endor to make their fortune in the galaxy. One of the best known is Joh Yowza, who won renown as a powerful, gravelly voiced vocalist for the Max Rebo Band.

PERSON OF INTEREST

WICKET

An inquisitive Ewok scout from Bright Tree Village, Wicket altered the course of galactic history when he encountered Leia Organa in the forests of Endor. Wicket helped persuade his tribe to fight alongside the rebels, and his bravery allowed the rebels to destroy the Death Star and defeat the Empire.

BRIGHT TREE VILLAGE

Histories of the Battle of Endor credit the Alliance's starfighter pilots, Pathfinder commandos and capital-ship crews for their decisive victory over the Empire. But their efforts would have been for naught without the Ewok warriors of Bright Tree Village, who saved the rebel command team sent to destroy the Death Star's shield generator. Decades later, Bright Tree Village remains a scattering of simple huts in the Endor treetops, with scavenged Imperial gear the only clues to its warriors' heroics.

MON MOTHMA

A former Republic and Imperial senator, Mon Mothma led the Alliance, overseeing often-fractious strategy meetings on Yavin 4 and preparations for a desperate strike at Endor.

BAGGAGE (STRAP) TAG
No. CHECKED Pcs. 02
Total Weight 11.38
To: Orig. Flt.
Transfer at: Transfer Flt.
Flight No. & Name:
END
FOREST MOON SPEEDER SERVICE
E-614-AVA
YUB NUB FOREST MOON SPEEDER SERVICE
ENDOR
No. CHECKED Pcs. 02
Total Weight 11.38

VEHICLES

HOME ONE

This MC80A star cruiser served as the Alliance's mobile headquarters after the disaster at Hoth, and was Admiral Ackbar's flagship for the Battle of Endor. When the Alliance became the New Republic, *Home One* remained at the center of the fight; Ackbar watched from its bridge as Imperial ships plowed into the surface of Jakku, a battle that marked the end of the Empire as a fighting force.

AT-ST

More nimble than the larger AT-AT, scout walkers are used for recon missions, patrols, and anti-personnel combat operations. Endor's Ewoks destroyed several with deadfalls and other improvised techniques.

74-Z SPEEDER BIKE

Aratech's 74-Z line was introduced during the Clone Wars, and its rugged, reliable design was largely unchanged during its decades of use by the Imperial military. On Endor, scout troopers used these bikes for recon and patrol missions, though the densely packed trees of the Sanctuary Moon's forests made for hazardous conditions at high speeds.

SIDE VIEW

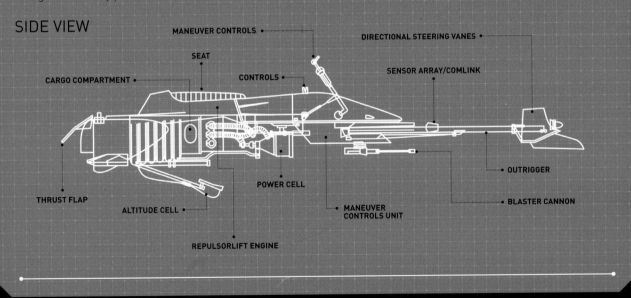

MANEUVER CONTROLS

DIRECTIONAL STEERING VANES

SEAT

CONTROLS

SENSOR ARRAY/COMLINK

CARGO COMPARTMENT

THRUST FLAP

ALTITUDE CELL

POWER CELL

REPULSORLIFT ENGINE

MANEUVER CONTROLS UNIT

OUTRIGGER

BLASTER CANNON

DROIDS

C-3PO

Built by Anakin Skywalker from scavenged parts, C-3PO served Padmé Amidala as a protocol droid then performed the same role for House Organa on Alderaan. Caught up in his friend R2-D2's secret rebel mission, he became a hero, albeit often a reluctant one. On Endor, he helped rally the Ewoks to support the rebels.

R2-D2

A plucky astromech, R2-D2 helped save Queen Amidala and her entourage from being destroyed by the Separatists blockade at Naboo, and assisted Anakin Skywalker as a starfighter pilot. Years later, he carried the Death Star plans, delivering them to the rebels on Yavin 4. Loyal and cool under fire, R2-D2 saved the lives of his friends innumerable times during their adventures.

FEATURE LOCATION

DEATH STAR II

Larger and packing more destructive power than its predecessor, the second Death Star also eliminated the vulnerable thermal exhaust port targeted by Yavin 4's rebel pilots. Emperor Palpatine leaked that the superweapon was being built above Endor to lure the Alliance into a battle there, but his plan backfired and he perished shortly before the station's demise.

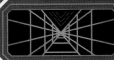

**STARKILLER
BASE**

PLANETARY DATA

SECTOR: 7G

TYPE: Terrestrial (Modified)

CLIMATE: Cold

DIAMETER: 660 km

TERRAIN: Mountains

ROTATION PERIOD: No Data

ORBITAL PERIOD: Not Applicable

SENTIENT SPECIES: None

POPULATION: No Data

STARKILLER BASE

THE NEW REPUBLIC REGARDED THE FIRST ORDER AS DEAD-ENDERS ON THE GALACTIC FRINGE, DISMISSING LEIA ORGANA'S WARNINGS THAT FLEETS AND ARMIES WERE TAKING SHAPE IN THE UNKNOWN REGIONS. SHE WAS PROVED CORRECT WHEN THE FIRST ORDER DECLARED WAR ON THE REPUBLIC BY REVEALING STARKILLER BASE, A SUPERWEAPON WHOSE FIRST SHOT INCINERATED HOSNIAN PRIME AND THE REPUBLIC SENATE FROM HALFWAY ACROSS THE GALAXY. STARKILLER BASE WAS A GROTESQUE CREATION, CARVED OUT OF A PLANET AND DRAINING SUNS FOR POWER. A RESISTANCE RAID DESTROYED STARKILLER, BUT THE REPUBLIC WAS LEFT LEADERLESS, WITH ONLY THE RESISTANCE LEFT TO OPPOSE THE FIRST ORDER'S MARCH.

OVERVIEW

COMMAND CENTRE • INTERROGATION ROOM
JUNCTION STATION • ASSEMBLY AREA
HANGAR 718

HISTORY

Resistance intel concluded that Starkiller Base siphoned "dark energy" from a star into its planetary core, unleashing it as a powerful beam tunnelling through hyperspace.

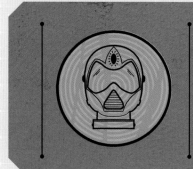

DK-RA-43'S COMMENT

"I hope we aren't visiting Starkiller Base, because there's nothing to visit. According to data from Resistance sources, Starkiller Base was destroyed in the vicinity of the Ilum system, leaving only debris, and its host sun was reduced to a cinder. The information I've gathered is speculative, including intel about key First Order commanders and military assets."

host planet gathered dark energy from a nearby star and stored it in a containment field at the planet core. A breach was then opened in the field, releasing destructive energy capable of tunneling through hyperspace.

ROGUES' GALLERY

KYLO REN

A warrior bearing a distinctive red-bladed lightsaber, Kylo Ren served as Supreme Leader Snoke's apprentice and enforcer, often clashing with General Armitage Hux as the First Order schemed to return to power. His origins were a mystery to most First Order officers, with few daring to seek the answers. He became Supreme Leader after Snoke's death.

GENERAL HUX

A fanatical believer in Imperial power, Armitage Hux was born on Arkanis to an Imperial officer who dreamed of creating an army of stormtroopers trained from birth. Armitage would help realize his father's plans and surpass him by becoming one of the First Order's foremost technologists and a ruthless leader.

CAPTAIN PHASMA

An imposing figure in chrome armor, Phasma was the final member of the triad that oversaw the First Order's day-to-day operations. She was in charge of the training program for stormtroopers, forging children into soldiers through relentless drills. The Resistance reports she died aboard Snoke's flagship shortly before the Battle of Crait.

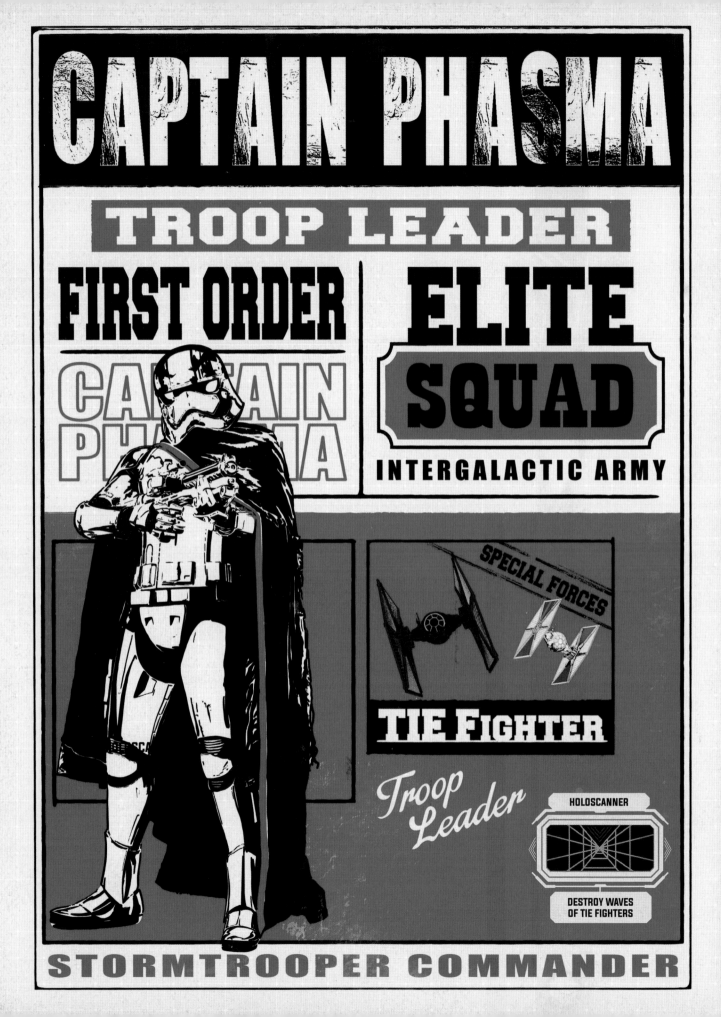

VEHICLES

FIRST ORDER SPECIAL FORCES TIE FIGHTER

The Empire saw its standard TIE fighters as disposable, refusing to outfit them with shields, but the First Order has rectified this deficiency in the standard TIE design. The new regime has also created a more powerful model, the TIE/sf, for use by its elite special forces. Special forces TIEs are flown by two pilots and boast both a heavy weapons turret and a hyperdrive.

POE DAMERON'S X-WING FIGHTER

The T-70 X-wing is part of the venerable line of X-wing starfighters, used since the days of the Rebel Alliance. While faster and more heavily armed than the T-65, the T-70 offers a similar combat profile, able to dogfight with enemy fighters or battle capital ships. The Resistance made do with T-70s donated by sympathizers in the New Republic, with Poe Dameron flying a distinctive ebon-hulled starfighter known as *Black One*.

STARKILLER BASE OSCILLATOR

Facing certain destruction, the Resistance sent agents and a fighter squadron to Starkiller Base in hopes of finding a weakness. After ground units brought down the base's shields, fighters blasted a hole in the armored housing of the thermal oscillator that controlled the network of generators maintaining Starkiller Base's containment field. When the oscillator ruptured, the containment field failed and its stored dark energy consumed both the weapon and the planet.

DROIDS

FIRST ORDER SENTRY DROID

Easily recognized by their distinctive white chassis, First Order sentry droids patrol the regime's starships and military installations, alert for intruders and any hint of dissent in the ranks.

FIRST ORDER INTERROGATION DROID

Developed in defiance of law from the New Republic, First Order IT-000 interrogation droids are programmed to extract intel from the regime's enemies, with no regard for the mental and physical scars left by their brutal methods.

WEAPONS

KYLO REN'S LIGHTSABER

Kylo's lightsaber is based on an ancient crossguard design with two quillons. A cracked kyber crystal leaves the blade unstable and shedding plasma embers.

FIRST ORDER F-11D BLASTER RIFLE

Sonn-Blas provides weapons to the First Order in defiance of New Republic law, with the F-11D proving the weapon of choice for new ranks of stormtroopers.

STARKILLER BASE

312

BATUU

PLANETARY DATA

SECTOR: Trilon

TYPE: Terrestrial

CLIMATE: Temperate

DIAMETER: 12,750 km

TERRAIN: Forests, mountains

ROTATION PERIOD: 24 standard hours

ORBITAL PERIOD: 365 local rotations

SENTIENT SPECIES: Humans

POPULATION: 200,000

EDGE OF THE GALAXY

BATUU

BATUU LIES ON THE GALACTIC
FRONTIER, SCANT PARSECS
FROM WILD SPACE AND THE
POORLY CHARTED STARS OF
THE TRILON SECTOR. IT'S A
TEMPERATE WORLD MARKED
BY DISTINCTIVE BLACK SPIRES
THAT RISE FROM ITS FORESTS. AN
ANCIENT SPECIES LEFT RUINS
ON BATUU BUT VANISHED LONG
BEFORE INTREPID EXPLORERS
REACHED THE PLANET. BATUU
HAS WELCOMED ARRIVALS
FROM MANY GALACTIC SPECIES,
AND DEVELOPED AN OPEN,
FRIENDLY CULTURE MELDING
MULTIPLE TRADITIONS. FOR
YEARS MOST ARRIVALS WERE
SMUGGLERS AND HYPERSPACE
SCOUTS, BUT AGENTS OF THE
FIRST ORDER, NEW REPUBLIC
AND THE RESISTANCE HAVE ALL
VISITED BLACK SPIRE OUTPOST
IN RECENT YEARS.

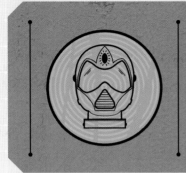

OVERVIEW

BLACK SPIRE OUTPOST • TRILON WISHING TREE • OLD OUTPOST • GALMA

HISTORY

Settlers came to Batuu eons ago – it was a thriving stop for traders before lightspeed technology was widely available – but booming hyperspace routes bypassed it, leaving it a backwater, and an ideal place for those who wanted (or needed) a quiet life. It is now a jumping-off point for adventures beyond the galactic frontier and Black Spire Outpost's spaceport features starship models from all across the galaxy. Known locally as BSO or the Spire, the outpost is Batuu's only major settlement, offering a spaceport, shops, and the chance to strike deals at Oga Garra's cantina. Arrivals at the Spire should change credits for spira (the local currency) and brush up on their Batuuan lingo: "Bright suns" is morning's greeting, "Rising moons" is evening's, and "Till the Spire" works as an all-purpose farewell.

HOLOSCANNER

UNLOCK THE
RISE OF SKYWALKER

INDEX